THE OTHER MAN

Conversations With Graham Greene

BOOKS BY

GRAHAM GREENE

NOVELS

The Man Within · Stamboul Train
It's a Battlefield · England Made Me · A Gun for Sale
Brighton Rock · The Confidential Agent
The Power and the Glory · The Ministry of Fear
The Heart of the Matter · The Third Man
The End of the Affair · Loser Takes All
The Quiet American · Our Man in Havana
A Burnt-Out Case · The Comedians · Travels with my Aunt
The Honorary Consul · The Human Factor
Dr Fischer of Geneva or The Bomb Party · Monsignor Quixote

SHORT STORIES

Collected Stories
(including *Twenty-one Stories, A Sense of Reality*
and *May We Borrow Your Husband?*)

TRAVEL

Journey Without Maps · The Lawless Roads
In Search of a Character

ESSAYS

Collected Essays · The Pleasure Dome · British Dramatists

PLAYS

The Living Room · The Potting Shed
The Complaisant Lover · Carving a Statue
The Return of A. J. Raffles · The Great Jowett

AUTOBIOGRAPHY

A Sort of Life · Ways of Escape

BIOGRAPHY

Lord Rochester's Monkey

FOR CHILDREN

The Little Fire Engine · The Little Horse Bus
The Little Steamroller · The Little Train

THE
OTHER MAN

Conversations With

GRAHAM GREENE

Marie-Françoise Allain

Translated from the French
by Guido Waldman

THE BODLEY HEAD
LONDON SYDNEY
TORONTO

British Library Cataloguing
in Publication Data
Greene, Graham
The other man: conversations with Graham Greene.
1. Greene, Graham—Biography
2. Authors, English—20th century—Biography
I. Title   II. Allain, Marie-Françoise
III. L'autre et son double. *English*
823'.912   PR6013.R44
ISBN 0-370-30468-3

Originally published in French as
L'Autre et son double
© Belfond 1981
Translation © The Bodley Head Ltd
and Simon & Schuster Inc 1983
Printed in Great Britain for
The Bodley Head Ltd
9 Bow Street, London WC2E 7AL
by William Clowes (Beccles) Ltd
Set in Monophoto Ehrhardt
First published in Great Britain 1983

CONTENTS

Preface by
Marie-Françoise Allain

A shadow always follows Graham Greene: that of another Graham Greene, who is and yet is not he. The ambiguity remains persistently, for he himself chooses concealment, out of modesty, a taste for secrecy, concern for his privacy, but most of all in order to protect from his own 'accidents of temperament' the one asset which he sees as essential—his work.

This book could be an admission of failure: in wanting to penetrate the recesses of this paradoxical personality, who is at once so remote from and so close to our time, one runs into a wall, a floating wall. Graham Greene does not volunteer confidences; he does not enjoy the sound of his own voice, he is not garrulous. He has discouraged the curious by insisting that anything he might say or write about his life or that could be said or written about it would be less revealing than his books.

However, he has agreed to be interviewed, which is exceptional enough. And he has talked, little by little, two steps forward, three steps back, evasive as ever. The long days of confrontation at Antibes in 1979, interrupted by more relaxed meals (without tape-recorder) chez Félix on the harbour, were succeeded by further weeks of 'interrogation' during which the writer applied himself to his role as interviewee. But this was no more than a role: Graham Greene is not a man to be exploited.

So he would remain concealed, on the pretext that he

had already written his autobiography, and that a volume of his articles and recollections was about to be published. Nevertheless, his reactions, his evasions were themselves revealing. Moreover he did occasionally indulge in frank speaking. Those wan replies, occasionally punctuated by an embarrassed laugh, conveyed indiscriminately the most trivial or incongruous fragment of life, as though the extremes in him were uniting in a mysterious attempt at reconciliation.

What we were faced with was not failure but a sort of painful prodigy.

And then suddenly, one November day in 1980, the other Graham Greene burst through his shadow. When the constraining play of question and answer was over, he decided to reveal himself by writing the Prologue and Dedication which follows. This final gesture gives a new dimension to the work. It is a way of shattering the anonymities, of short-circuiting the classic mechanisms, of rehabilitating 'the human factor'. It reveals Graham Greene as much as the rest of the book does: this becomes almost tangibly the point of contact between the mythical writer, slinking by in his nineteen-thirties raincoat, and the man who is moved (not without a twinge of pain) to assert his right to loyalties, even to divided loyalties.

MARIE-FRANÇOISE ALLAIN

Prologue and Dedication

MARIE-FRANÇOISE ALLAIN: *You are reputed not to like interviews. Why have you consented to do this book with me?*

GRAHAM GREENE: Because I see you more as a literary critic than a journalist. But far more important in my view, because you're the daughter of Yves Allain, and I'm proud to have been his friend. He was a professional in the world of espionage; it's a world where I've never been anything but a minor cog, an amateur for a few years during the war, but I shared your pain and distress when he disappeared and was subsequently found assassinated in Morocco—an assassination which will no doubt always remain a mystery. Can we both dedicate this book to his memory?

I should never have dared to provoke such a gesture. I am very grateful to you.

I attended his strange funeral in Paris in November 1966, along with another mutual friend, and we realized that there were, in and around the church, as many undercover men, *barbouzes*, as mourners. Your mother later told me that the driver of the hearse which brought his body back to Brittany had hinted that he was one himself. Yves had been decorated by my government for his great services to the Resistance, and I wrote a letter of tribute and sent it to *The Times*, but it wasn't published. When I asked why not, the editor answered that, according to his correspondent, there was no official trace in Paris of Yves Allain's assassination. The Elysée had apparently issued instructions to the press that no further allusion was to be made to the circumstances of his death, which had already been kept hidden, even from his family, for the last seven days and more. When I told *The Times* that this correspondent of theirs couldn't have taken the trouble to read *Le Figaro* or *Le Monde* of 8 and 9 November 1966, the editor unobtrusively published my modest tribute. If you happen still to have this *Times* cutting in your possession, let us take the liberty of reproducing it here in his memory.

For my English critics, my novels take place in a distant and exotic world which they call 'Greeneland'. Well, Paris isn't very far from London, and Paris was certainly a part of this 'exotic' world on that sinister day of your father's funeral.

Have you ever thought of writing a book about my father's death?

I've thought of it many times. When he disappeared, I made notes of the lies which were told me and of the moral blackmail exerted on you by French Radio-Television, who were his official employers; but the circumstances of his death have remained deeply buried, in Morocco as in France, and the long and possibly dangerous task of discovering the truth must fall to some younger writer.

YVES ALLAIN

Mr Graham Greene writes:

The brutal murder of Yves Allain in Morocco less than two weeks after his arrival to take up the position of Chief of Post for the O.R.T.F. Rabat will come as a shock to his many English friends. He was a man of great courage, loyalty and integrity, how much courage was shown very early, when he was hardly out of college, as one of the *grands résistants* in Brittany. He directed the famous

Bourgogne escape network to which some 250 Allied airmen owed their freedom, and he personally accompanied to the Spanish border many men who spoke not a word of French. He received as his British award a modest M.B.E. like so many heroes and heroines of the Resistance; his French decorations included the Croix de Guerre with palm, the Medal of the Resistance and the Légion d' Honneur and his American the Medal of Freedom.

The Times, 24 November 1966

I

The Secret Man

'It's for others to discover the picture ...'

Since he tends to see himself as one of his characters, and the outlines of the characters in his novels seem to be studiedly imprecise, the portrait I sketch out here will reflect in only a shadowy and no doubt clumsy way the 'moments of agony' which these interviews initially represented for him.

But Greene at all events remains obscure in his life, his work, his person. So he keeps his interlocutor or reader in a dilemma, hoping to discover him and yet reluctant to pursue a frustrating investigation. He is impressive, restless, occasionally frivolous, subject to sudden tempers and to almost child-like enthusiasms; he resembles a stick of Brighton rock which, by definition, reveals the name of Brighton no matter where you break it. The fact is that, whatever the question he was prepared to answer, whether he was talking about Cuba or Indo-China, the lawless roads of Mexico, the fleshpots of Brighton, or indeed his childhood Berkhamsted, the name GRAHAM GREENE has always featured, like a signature, in his answer. As he grew more familiar, he grew more perplexing.

Puzzled by this sense of being at home in an unfamiliar world, one quickly realizes that it is not a question of his name being written all too boldly; what is emphasized is his grey universe of second-rate journalists, small-time crooks with a habit of evil, unfulfilled actors, poor sods—like the rest of us. He carries this around with him in addition to his own neuroses—his obsession with escape (the verb 'to escape' keeps recurring in his conversation), his attraction towards 'the dangerous edge of things', the duality which has marked his life.

Thus the dialogue is impregnated with a complex and almost tender note of anguish. Anguish is the dominant tone; it gives way only to a sense of the absurd and of the ridiculous, the outcome of an immense self-control.

Anguish and self-control are two contrasting elements reflecting the internal dissensions of Graham Greene.

'There's another man within me that's angry with me.'
Sir Thomas Browne
(Epigraph to *The Man Within*)

So you do not like yourself . . .
No, but then how many people do like themselves, if they stop to think of it? I am not at ease with myself, it's true—but I don't regard this as a fault. Besides, how can one be at ease with oneself?

Did psycho-analysis not help you?
I was sixteen at the time. It did help me in the sense that I escaped for a few months from the school at Berkhamsted, where I was quite miserable. In London, I lived like a lord at my analyst's, Kenneth Richmond. A maid brought me breakfast in bed. I came and went as I pleased. I attended to my studies in Kensington Gardens, and devoted precisely one hour a day to the telling of my dreams. I kept a dream-diary, (I still do occasionally). I met all sorts of people at Richmond's, writers for the most part. I lived a civilized life, far from the barbarity of school.

I think this was what helped me rather than the analysis itself, which came nowhere near to sorting me out.

At all events I still don't know myself, for I have no wish to know myself. I'm somewhat in the situation of Rainer Maria Rilke, who was afraid of psycho-analysis. He said he was frightened that it might clear everything up, to the detriment of his unconscious mind—the part of the mind which nourishes creativity.

I think it's unhealthy to dwell on the negative side of one's own character, as analysis and auto-analysis inevitably do; they reinforce the Christian concept of guilt. It is never one's positive side that comes to light.

Are you worried about having too often to beat your breast?

Not at all! In fact I don't think I'm really all that interested in myself. I have been far more interested in other people, ever since I was a child. I'm much less bothered by the failures and successes in my own life than by those of my invented characters. This way I manage to escape—from myself, I mean.

There is somewhere in here a double contradiction. In 1971 you wrote your autobiography, A Sort of Life, *which suggests at least a momentary self-concern; you also took the occasion to confess 'I see myself as one of my characters.'*

That's true. I still think, though, that one has to avoid being dominated by a character, becoming attached to it or too involved in it, even if that character happens to be oneself.

As for the autobiography, you mustn't forget that I began it as a form of therapy. I had no work in progress. I was suffering from one of my acute depressions. I'd gone to a psychiatrist friend to demand electric-shock treatment, but what he said was, 'Bear with your depression for another fortnight. Meanwhile start writing down what you remember of your childhood.' I did what he told me. The fortnight passed, my depression too (without shock treatment), and I had written a good number of pages which later turned into the opening of *A Sort of Life*: the first twenty-five years, or even sixteen, provide a rich enough quarry to exploit for the rest of life. I consigned the memories to a drawer to start with—I had no intention of turning them into an autobiography.

Your autobiography ends, rather strangely, after the publication of Stamboul Train, *when you were about twenty-eight. In your preface you explain that 'any conclusion must be arbitrary' and you have 'preferred to finish this essay with the years of failure which followed the acceptance of my first novel'. Why end on a failure?*

Because failure is also 'a sort of death', a normal stopping-point. My life is marked by a succession of failures which left their traces on my work. I think they're the warp and weft of it. Besides, I didn't want to involve the living in my work—I feel I have no right to do that, any more than I wanted to usurp the rights vested in other people's lives when I published the recollections and articles collected in *Ways of Escape*. Their lives are *their* property, not mine; so *Ways of Escape* was not an autobiography but a selection of news stories which I wrote in Malaya, Kenya and so on, together with a handful of personal anecdotes. I had no wish to renew the experiment of *A Sort of Life*. I hate brooding on the past. The book, though, does have enough material to fill some gaps (if possible!) in certain periods of my life.

A life is, after all, a pretty chaotic affair—and I'm not thinking just of my own life but of the one which goes on around us. During the First World War I was old enough to realize what was happening. My father was always reading the paper to find out how many of his Old Boys had been killed in the course of the week. Then we lived through the Second World War, and I think we were all strongly impressed with the sense of chaos. After that revolutions, guerrilla warfare ... disorder rather than an evil fate. Upheavals in South America, *coups d'état*, terrorism. We're part of this world, aren't we? We're affected by this sort of life. We're at the heart of the disorder.

But you do not like order ...

I don't like imposed or established order, but I imagine that every writer aims at some sort of organization: he composes order with the help of his characters, he tries to plan lives. Invention is a form of organization. However, I wouldn't dream of dividing my life into periods—that's for the critics to do. I consider that in spite of the prevailing chaos, my life is a relatively coherent whole, at least in so far as my books are concerned, with one or two exceptions. I suppose one might work out an overall structure for it, though I can't see to what purpose.

At this moment a person hitherto unknown to me, Norman Sherry, is busy writing my biography. The poor man! Terrible things keep happening to him as he goes wherever I've been. He dogs my footsteps. He's been to the same lost Mexican villages. He's caught dysentery in the very Mexican town where I caught it in 1938. He's gone to Liberia forty-five years after me, and in the very country where I almost died of fever, he barely avoided the revolution. He plans to go to the leper colony I visited in the Congo in 1959. My experiences are certainly giving him plenty to do. I'm glad this biography is being written by a non-Catholic: it will, I hope, be more objective.

... so far as your adventurous side is concerned. But what traces do you leave of your 'inner journeys'?

The two are connected. If he does not recognize me in my writer's role, it's still me he recognizes, but in a different role. We each contain several characters—I don't fight them, I accept them. To find an 'integrated' person one would have to look in a lunatic asylum. As for my 'inner journeys', I doubt whether anything I, or anyone else, could say or write about me would reveal as much as my books.

So you really are 'Greene-ian'?

It's a term I can't stand, any more than the word 'Greeneland'. I don't believe in it, I can't make it out. So don't go asking me to explain myself. I don't know myself, and I don't want to. Don't try to trap me with some sentence I wrote thirty to fifty years ago, expecting me to think the same way today. I am, remember, someone who changes. Each year I feel different.

That corroborates (if you will permit me) what you wrote when you said, 'my roots are in rootlessness ...'; or, again, what you confided to a journalist, 'I don't want to stay in one place too long in case the ice melts beneath my feet'!

Fate willed me to be a writer, and I write about rootlessness. That is my subject, in a way.

Is there not a paradox between the freedom deriving from an absence of roots, and the weight of destiny, about which you often speak?

None that I can see. Don't you believe many writers have this sense of some ineluctable force driving them to write? Isn't it true of every vocation? If I were a doctor or a priest, wouldn't I also feel as though a rope were tightening round my neck?

My subject is rootlessness—but then my subject matter is my life, so there's no paradox. The other day a critic suggested that I could not feel at home anywhere as I was forever globe-trotting. I replied that in fact I feel at home wherever I am. During my 'retreat' in the leper colony at Yonda I did feel a sense of being out of my element—for about half an hour. Then, when I had been assigned a little hut, and had met the leper boy who was to look after me, and had left a few books on the table along with a note-pad; when I'd embarked on a regular round, punctuated by my morning strolls down to the Congo, followed by my visits to Dr Lechat's dispensary—I felt quite at home. I expect my words about the ice melting beneath my feet were just a sally. One might detect in them perhaps a hint of truth, a superficial hint. Rootlessness is not my problem.

So it is only in relation to yourself that you feel off balance?
Yes. What I said in my autobiography, about the epigraph I should choose for every novel I've written, remains true: 'Our interest's on the dangerous edge of things.'[1] 'The dangerous edge of things' remains what it always has been—the narrow boundary between loyalty and disloyalty, between fidelity and infidelity, the mind's contradictions, the paradox one carries within oneself. This is what men are made of. In *A Burnt-Out Case*, for instance, Dr Colin is an atheist, but he ponders on the origins of human kind, while the priests with whom he rubs shoulders seem less mystical than he, preoccupied as they are with building shelters for the lepers or raising money for their hospital. It's all a paradox and that's what interests me.

In constantly grazing 'the dangerous edge of things' have you never been tempted to make the leap?
Yes indeed, and this is precisely why I'm a committed person. I'm bound by certain ideas, though not by any clear political line. I've often felt a strong pull towards the

[1] 'Our interest's on the dangerous edge of things.
   The honest thief, the tender murderer,
   The superstitious atheist, demireps
   That love and save their souls in new French books –
   We watch while these in equilibrium keep
   The giddy line midway.'
                    ROBERT BROWNING: *Bishop Blougram's Apology*

Communist party (but never towards the extreme Right). I shouldn't be a good recruit, though, for my loyalty would change with circumstances, if I judged that the party had made a mistake. So I would find myself frequently disobeying and stepping out of line!

How is it that you once admired Kim Philby precisely because of the constancy with which he served Communism, in spite of Stalin and Stalinism?

One admires qualities one does not possess oneself. Philby really lived out his loyalty. I like this monolithic quality of his.

Do you mean that you yourself are quite two-sided, that you are 'lapsed'?

How is one to know? Before the pontificate of John XXIII, the Holy Office condemned *The Power and the Glory*. I was considered an undesirable Catholic, practically a heretic. Many people might then have said that I had 'lapsed'; in their eyes the precarious balance had been upset—but not in mine.

When have you 'lapsed' in your own eyes?

I've perpetrated some bad books. I don't like *The Heart of the Matter*, though it was the start of my success, back in 1949. That is speaking of literature. Politically speaking, I'm not conscious of having overbalanced either in favour of the Communists or of anyone else. As for the human aspect ... Well, there I've failed time and again. Yes, on the human plane there have been plenty of failures, no doubt about it: I've betrayed a great number of things and people in the course of my life, which probably explains this uncomfortable feeling I have about myself, this sense of having been cruel, unjust. It still torments me often enough before I go to sleep.

Then where is the 'icicle' which you discovered early in life, and which is lodged 'in the heart of the writer'?

It's still there. I think that's what provokes cruelty—and afterwards one realizes that it's too late. It resurfaces in each *mea culpa*.

You choose the term mea culpa. *Are you afraid of hell?*

No: I don't believe in it. I believe, rather in a sort of purgatory.

What is purgatory?

It's what we—you and I—are living through at this moment.

You did write to me that in this interview we should be experiencing some moments of 'agony'. Is that not rather a strong term?

I exaggerated a little—but it's not easy to give straight answers to your questions, answers which are neither too ambiguous nor too evasive. Normally one isn't concerned with analyzing oneself, still less with discussing oneself.

You say 'one', not 'I'. Why is that?

Yes, I know; it's a habit, one of those tics I often have to suppress when I'm writing. I suppose I don't like being too personal. In the collection of articles contained in *Ways of Escape*, I never wanted to use the first person; as a result, in my new version I have had to suppress all the *ones* even though they're more precise than *we*, with its connotation of several individuals sharing an identical view of things. *One* presupposes a single individual—a more abstract one, I'll grant you. I'll admit, too, that it's a way of escaping from myself.

You observe in one of your essays that the intellect strives to be impersonal. Are you always trying to dissimulate?

Is it dissimulation, or simply a desire not to overstress what is purely personal? I don't know.

A theme in your life, and in your work, is escape from yourself; is this not so?

(21)

Yes; and today's theme is more a facing up to oneself, isn't it?

Not necessarily. It could give a further occasion, a further means to continue to construct a certain image of yourself which you wish to convey!

But I've no wish to present any image of myself—least of all a false one.

So there does exist somewhere or other a true image?

That's for others to discover, not me. I expect you're familiar with Henry James's words about 'the pattern in the carpet'. In any body of work there's always a pattern to be found. Well, *I* don't want to see it. When a critic discovers certain keynotes, that's fine and may be of interest, but I don't want to be steeped in his discoveries, I want to remain unaware of them. Otherwise I think my imagination would dry up. For the same reason I never re-read my books; I know I would come across all too many repetitions due quite simply to forgetting what I had written before. I've not the slightest wish to have my nose rubbed onto 'the pattern in the carpet'.

Critics have remarked, in this context, that I'm a one-book man. They're right, up to a point, though I would say I was a two- or three-book man, for I've several times managed to alter the keynote, to disrupt the pattern. I'm thinking of *Travels with my Aunt*, where I took a rest from myself—as I also did in *Doctor Fischer of Geneva*, and perhaps, on reflection, in one or two other cases.

What do you mean by 'taking a rest from yourself'?

Freeing myself from familiar characters and from myself. I always watch my characters very closely and this generates a considerable tension. For instance, in *A Burnt-Out Case*, I lived with a neurotic, Querry, and his presence affected me in the smallest of humdrum details—a little as though an actor playing the part of Othello suddenly

(22)

realized that he was behaving like Othello in his private life. The bond between the character and the self is so strong, it can have some disastrous effects on one's own life.

You certainly seem to be so close to your heroes that one inevitably identifies you with various of them.

Surely not! They're all so different! Am I identified with Pinkie, the murderer in *Brighton Rock*, or with Harry Lime, the appalling trafficker in *The Third Man*?

Oh but yes! Paul Theroux remarks à propos of the 'mystery' you represent, that you could be 'an archbishop and a criminal' both at the same time.

He was speaking of my physical appearance, if I remember rightly. Say what you will, I doubt whether any parallel can be drawn between Pinkie, Harry Lime and myself!

Well, no—but can it not, perhaps, with the 'whisky priest' in The Power and the Glory?

There perhaps you're nearer the truth!

What truth is that?

I don't know. I'm the last person who can say what the truth is about me. At all events I don't think that in our present situation I would try to lie or to conceal myself from you, because you're a friend, not a journalist.

During a brief period of my life I had, for personal reasons, to train myself to lie. Falsehood became a protection—it afforded me several 'covers'. And with journalists I certainly do cheat. This has nothing to do with my few years in Intelligence during World War Two: I think I would have always dealt this way with journalists, even without that experience—I don't like people plundering my private life. It has nothing to do, either, with my personality. It's simply that I don't like people regarding me as a source of articles written for their own profit.

But you have always had a taste for secrecy or for whatever is secret. You may look like a quiet Englishman, or an archbishop or a criminal, but I have never seen a man change faces so often, without 'batting an eyelid'. It is a little discouraging!

Really? And yet I'm constantly being told that I have only two masks: Boredom and Amusement!

Even those who know you well have a feeling that you are hiding something, that you 'have complete control of a situation, both in what you say and in the way you look'. One of your friends has observed that your eyes were like a blind man's: 'You can't be sure whether you are looking right through them or they are looking right through you.'[1] This leaves an impression of quiet anguish which is very hard to endure.

What you take for anguish is, I think, no more than a slight case of bulging eyes! When I was in hospital with appendicitis at twenty-one or -two, I was given milk with iodine because they said I was suffering from some sort of ophthalmic goitre; my brother, who was a doctor, laughed when he heard this, and said it was ridiculous. The fact remains that my eyes bulge! At all events I'm anxious to know whether I'll be able to answer your questions, not as you or I want me to, but with honesty.

As for my peaceable appearance, I very often am at peace. But 1979 has not been a year of serenity: I was ill and, given my age, people assumed that *The Human Factor* was to be my last book, so they gave me no peace—it was a nightmare. But I'm particularly serene when I'm on holiday, or rather when I'm at work! At this moment I'm not working and I'm not enjoying a peaceful period. I want

[1] *Graham Greene at 75*, produced by Philip French for the BBC, 1 October 1979, with Anthony Burgess, John Le Carré, Graham Greene, Sir Hugh Greene, Michael Meyer, Dilys Powell, V. S. Pritchett, Sir Ralph Richardson and Paul Theroux.

to go to Capri; there I find peace, deep peace, especially if I'm at work on a book. I believe I've said in one of my prefaces and I still maintain, that I can't see how anyone who does not write, paint or compose can get through life at all. Writing is a sort of therapy—the way one writes, but also the experiences, the events in one's life which provide, however remotely, the basis for one's writing. Those articles I wrote in Kenya in 1953 during the Mau Mau rebellion, or in Malaya during the Emergency, had their dangerous sources, to say the least, but the danger offered the possibility of escape from the grisly routine of daily life, just as the theatre has offered me the chance to dissipate the loneliness of writing. The means of escaping the humdrum, or of escaping the crises which can arise in one's emotional life, have been quite varied. Of course nowadays certain exits are closed to me. A few years ago I was asked to go to Belfast for *The Catholic Herald*, and I told them I was too old to get myself killed. I don't think that I could today go out and cover anything equivalent to the Mau Mau rebellion. There are fewer substitutes for dangerous living. So I go on writing: the escaper's royal road—it always has been.

Why escape?

Because I don't like myself.

In all my books perhaps I return to the duality which has marked my life from the time that I was a pupil in the school at Berkhamsted whose head was my father. Hence my 'divided loyalties': I had friends, a few, but I was also my father's son—and they disliked my father. I belonged to neither side. I couldn't side with the boys without betraying my father, and they regarded me like a collaborator in occupied territory. I made obvious use of these divided loyalties in the person of the priest in *The Power and the Glory.* In *The Heart of the Matter*, a book I dislike, Scobie is torn between pity and pride. In *The Third Man* one could probably find this theme of friendship betrayed, but betrayed in a better cause. Even Sarah, in *The End of the Affair*, remains torn between her love for Bendrix and her love, her sudden electrifying love, for God.

Thanks to these books I've recaptured my experience of childhood, or rather of that part of it when I was a boarder, at twelve or thirteen. I've had no wish to do away with this cleavage; I've accepted it as one of the constants of my work and of my life. Perhaps it was the only way to exorcize the evil, for there's no doubt, it was a most unpleasant situation.

You even went as far as to make an astounding assertion in a footnote to A Sort of Life; *'I couldn't bear mentally living again for several years in these [school] surroundings. A leper colony in the Congo was preferable ...' What was so horrible about it to justify such a comparison?*

The sense of inevitable betrayal. Being caught between two fires, I was ostracized, I found myself in the situation of a leper.

What meaning do you attach to this image of a leper?

It is quite a familiar image in literature.

Is it nothing more for you?

Well, it's easy enough to interpret, though perhaps it has other meanings. In the Middle Ages the leper had to ring his bell when approaching people. And I wrote (or said once?) that innocence is like a leper with his bell. Innocence is not to be trusted.

Why innocence?

Innocence and pity. Innocence can be exceedingly foolish, disastrous—like that of Pyle, the quiet American.

I still do not understand how you associate leprosy and innocence.

(26)

Remember, it was 'In the lost boyhood of Judas/Christ was betrayed'.[1] Judas, finally, was innocent. It was a child's innocence which carried betrayal.

Perhaps I should never have said I felt like a leper but rather like a Quisling (the Norwegian minister who collaborated with the Nazis); a divided loyalty or the betrayal of one's own loyalty.

In 1959, after three months in the Congo leper colony, I had a dream. I dreamed of a leper in Sweden—yes, Sweden, not Norway. He went to see an old professor of medicine, who shut the door in his face with the advice that he should seek treatment at a clinic. The leper begged him for help; he would lose his job if his disease became public knowledge. The professor replied severely that Swedish law forbade his treating a leper outside a hospital. Then the poor man came back at night and knocked at the Herr Professor's door. And suddenly everything had changed; an officer had turned up in the course of the day and said to the doctor, 'Listen, we're giving a party to celebrate the seventieth birthday of our retired General. As Swedish law forbids gambling, we should like to turn your house into a casino just for tonight. It will give the General such a thrill—he used to love playing roulette at Monte Carlo. We'll take care of everything. We'll bring an orchestra, we'll provide the tables, just for the night. The old General will be so pleased!' The professor eventually consented.

So when the leper dragged himself across the fields that night to see the professor and beg him to treat him in secret, the house was totally transformed. There were lights, laughter, cigar smoke ... Well, while a champagne cork was gaily popping from a bottle the leper shot himself

---

[1] From *Germinal* By A.E., quoted by Graham Greene in his essay *The Lost Childhood*.

through the forehead with a revolver. And I've asked myself as I've pondered over this dream of a strange country: 'Am I the professor, or the leper?'

A little of each I think.

Once again, a double-agent . . .

II

Divided Loyalties

'To go back far in time is always a painful experience (as one approaches death one lives a step ahead, perhaps in a hurry to be gone).'[1] The snatches of childhood memories had therefore to be wrested from him as though he took little interest in his past, as though he were still stirring up so much pain that he preferred to come striding into the present.

In these dialogues it is difficult to convey the passion, almost the horror evoked by his recollection of life at boarding school; when I expressed surprise, he cried, 'But it was horrible ... The promiscuity, the total absence of solitude, there was the horror.'

The humiliations, the enforced duplicity (his own) are smelt for a moment like the stench from a prison-cell, reminding one of a hunted man, stalked even by his shadow, a 'pathological case'. He has admitted to never having had deliberate recourse to memory unless he was forced to it, as in the present circumstances. He claims that he is more inclined to remember what he has not written—but the questions tended to concentrate on those parts of his distant past which had been as it were 'flushed out' in his autobiography. He no longer wanted to remember because, once a life had been consigned to paper, it was to

[1] Introduction to *It's a Battlefield* in the Collected Edition.

be forgotten—forgotten, not reconstructed. So while these two prime reasons seem to have led to the details of his childhood being erased, the determining factors in his adult life are none the less preserved: the indefinable childhood happiness, the boredom, the excessive despair, the obsession to write, and especially that all-pervading double allegiance whose roots he was beginning to uncover.

'Divided loyalty' made its appearance between childhood and adolescence. What was there before?

A state of happiness. My childhood was extremely peaceful until thirteen, when I was taken away from home and sent to boarding school. My father was still on hand, as he was our headmaster, but the contrast was all the sharper because I had always known him in a happy atmosphere within a large family. We were self-sufficient—six brothers and sisters and six cousins who lived only a few hundred yards away: so there were twelve of us children of varying ages.

At Berkhamsted the Greenes were very numerous. They represented practically one per cent of the population, for you had to allow not only for the dozen children and their four parents but also for several aunts. We didn't need anyone else.

This 'tribal' happiness does not appear to have left any traces in your memory. Those years appear as a deserted beach rather than as a tangible space.

The days flowed into each other, and so did the weeks, interrupted only by short holidays by the seaside, or by this and that. Even these trivial interruptions were repetitious, but then happiness is repetitious, while pain is marked by crises which sear the memory. Happiness survives only in the odd incident. Being happy is almost like making love:

one attains a state of blissful 'nothing'—one does not remember, one remembers only happiness, a state of contentment.

We were happy.

This torment, then, this anguish, this sense of failure which is so poignant in your books—where does it come from?

From my adolescence, between thirteen and sixteen, when I started trying to escape from myself. It's all bound up with boredom, I think. Boredom started impinging when I was about sixteen. It reached a point where I felt I had a balloon blowing up inside my head, ready to burst. It was something physical as well as mental, something in the head which was going to crack, to blast it to smithereens. Whenever this happened, I'd persuade my elder brother to take me to London, to browse in the second-hand book-shops, so as to derive from this minimal change of rhythm at least a temporary respite.

I was bored. In the eighteenth century they called it 'spleen'. We have in English a long poem entitled *Spleen*.[1] I've never read it and can't remember who wrote it . It was a common disease at the time.

I suppose it did not affect people as active as you are?

Who knows whether it wasn't spleen that drove Scott towards the Antarctic? Well before I was sixteen I wanted to explore the Antarctic too. Only the Antarctic—the North Pole didn't interest me; it was only a continent of ice compared to the South Pole with its high plateaux. I remember, when I was about fourteen, I wrote a little note to an explorer called Bruce, criticizing his book, *Polar Exploration*, in the Home University Library. He replied with a most charming letter. I can't remember what I

[1] By Matthew Green, 1696–1737.

found to criticize. I imagined, in spite of my loathing for uniforms (I was never a Boy Scout), that if I became a Sea Scout I might join a polar expedition.

Had you already considered leaving home before you were thirteen?

I don't think so. I didn't need to; my parents showed so little curiosity about my private life. My mother was very remote and showed no interest in our affairs. You saw a little notebook in which she began noting down my age when I started to walk, my children's illnesses, etc. She soon gave it up—I suppose it bored her. But I never suffered from her indifference. I was very fond of her, though I realized that I could go happily for months without seeing her. The feeling must have been mutual. We were devoted to each other but from a distance—that was part of the educational system in those days. Besides, we had plenty of servants, and she had her hands full with her brood.

My father, too, was fully occupied; he was Headmaster, but he also did duty as Housemaster, with twenty or thirty boarders in his charge. One of the school buildings, called School House, harboured the boarders. My father delegated to my mother the responsibility for the catering and domestic arrangements.

As children we went down to the drawing room from the nursery around five in the afternoon and stayed with my mother till seven. She would read to us. Then we would choose a game from our imposing array of pastimes. We had a nursemaid and a nanny—it was a very different life, that of the upper middle classes in those days.

I've always appreciated the fact that my mother was not possessive. I loved her all the more for that.

You say little about your father.

I had no feelings about him. He embodied Authority too

much, and kept asking me irritating questions like, 'Did you have a nice evening at X's?' or, 'Did the concert go on late?' I started to grow fond of him when I was an adult, while I was up at Balliol. I think I behaved a bit roughly towards him then, for he was very liberal—not only in the political sense, belonging as he did to the Liberal Party—but in the true liberal sense, while I was being tempted by extremes: I mean the Communist Party, with which I flirted briefly. In 1923 one could still believe in the October Revolution.

'The dangerous edge of things'?

No; my Party membership lasted four weeks and fizzled out completely. I consider it no more than a joke.

I had glimpsed the dangerous edge of things much earlier, even before playing Russian roulette. The horror began at thirteen. The school world really was horrible. There was no privacy. The wc doors could not be locked: the boys never stopped farting around me. I lived in a scatological world. In those dormitories life was very innocent: I never had any homosexual problem, no more as victim than as aggressor. Perhaps this was just my naïvety, for I later discovered that one of my best school-friends, who was at Oxford with me, was a homosexual. I'd never noticed it before; probably I had too much else on my mind, for at all events he showed no leanings towards me—we were simply friends. Actually I found out without realizing it, quite naturally, when I was eighteen or so. The discovery didn't surprise me or shock me.

Was it not a case of late maturing? You have sometimes been suspected of ambiguity even in this area, especially in the slant of your books.

Ambiguity may exist, perhaps, if one looks for it; but I have never engaged in homosexuality.

Is this not strange, for a man drawn towards duality?

(33)

No, it never attracted me or interested me. A few homo-
sexuals may be found in *May We Borrow Your Husband?*,
but they've left scarcely a trace in my life or in my novels.
One of my best friends, Evelyn Waugh, used to tease me
about this; he claimed that I had lost a great deal by not
going through a homosexual phase, just as he had at Oxford.
I fear, though, that in this area I've been abnormally normal.

*You say you have always been very sensitive to smell, a
'power infinitely more evocative than sounds and perhaps even
than things seen'. This no doubt explains your revulsion for the
scatological atmosphere pervading the dormitories. But it does
not seem to explain your use of the word 'horrible' in this
context, or of the word 'humiliation' which you use in* A Sort
of Life. *And yet I know how you weigh your words!*

But it *was* 'horrible'. I think I've always needed privacy.
The promiscuity, the total absence of solitude—there was
the horror.

Would not a leper or a Quisling necessarily enjoy such solitude?

Perhaps, during school hours, but that still left life as a
boarder. I admit I was a pathological case. I took drastic
measures to survive.

*Measures against yourself? Was not that the moment when
your behaviour became almost demented, like cutting your leg
with a pen-knife?*

Oh, that was just to get myself excused gym, to hobble
myself! The motive was clear enough.

And the perfectly sound tooth you had extracted?

That was much later, after Oxford. The ether gave me a
few moments' respite from boredom.

*You desired solitude, but at the same time you mention this
terrible sense of ostracism which afflicted you. Just what did
you want?*

Solitude has never bothered me. I've done most of my
travelling alone. Emotional loneliness didn't worry me

(34)

either. I loved and admired my mother precisely because she never trespassed on my privacy.

There was probably some trauma when I was taken away from my family. I could scarcely stand my school-fellows or children of my age. I had my sisters and my brothers, who were all I needed. Today I'm still very close to my younger sister and my younger brother.

And your children?

Well, not in that sense. I think my books are my children. I'm very fond of my son and daughter; but just as I didn't want my parents meddling in my private life, I don't want to intrude into theirs. I simply want to be there if they need me. The only period of enforced separation from my children was when they were small, during the war. I evacuated them to Oxford, while I was in London, then Sierra Leone, then London again. It had to be so; first London was under the Blitz, then the V.1's and the V.2's, and I was working for MI6 from 1941 to '44.

Do you not feel guilty when you confess that your books are your children?

Not in the least. Perhaps it's an unfortunate admission, but it's every writer's obsession, and it will out. I'm not a part-timer!

I'm sure I didn't initially make a conscious choice of isolation. I don't know what induced me to conceal from my parents the fact that I could read. It may have been an innate penchant for secrecy, or it may have been a very rational fear of their realizing that I was big enough to be thrown into the world of school. I was six or seven—very late for my age. I remember when I received an honorary degree at Cambridge, I met an old scholar who was receiving the same award with me—Dr Dover Wilson, the greatest living authority on Shakespeare. He had known my parents; he turned to me and whispered, 'To think that

(35)

they were so worried about you because you were taking so long to learn to read!' I had managed to keep it a secret for a few months ... until the day when my mother gave me a book to pass the time on a train journey, and I kept it shut too obviously, fixing my eye with suspicious obstinacy on the cover with its colour illustration.

Later, this impulse towards introversion would drive me to spend hours hiding on Berkhamsted Common. I was a past master in the art of playing truant. Banishment, whether enforced or voluntary, has certainly sparked the theme of escape in my books, as in *The Man Within* and even in my first, unpublished, novel which dealt with the black child of white parents, who was himself a black sheep.

Have you suffered in your friendships? What are these 'humiliations' that one guesses at?

I don't know what you mean by 'humiliations' without the context.

Was it not connected with the treachery of your friend Carter?

The traitor was someone else. What Carter did was practise moral torture to perfection, because I was the headmaster's son. I forget the name of the boy who deserted me in order to join forces with Carter. I know I chanced upon him at Kuala Lumpur on my return from a three-day expedition into the jungle in 1951. As a child I brooded on revenge. Now it no longer mattered in the least. Why speak of 'humiliation', then? Do we have to check it?[1]

---

[1] Each time I quoted his own words back to him, Graham Greene checked the reference with me, if he did not recognize it, in order to avoid errors of interpretation. As it happened, referring in *A Sort of Life* to Watson's disloyalty, he wrote: 'I wondered ... if I would ever have written a book had it not been for Watson and the dead Carter, if those years of humiliation had not given me an excessive desire to prove that I was good at something ...'

I do not know. If this sentiment exists somewhere deep within you, there is no need.

No, I don't feel it any more. Writing *A Sort of Life*, you see, was in the nature of a psycho-analysis. I made a long journey through time, and I was one of my characters, as you have said. So the emotions I felt at the time are not necessarily reawakened. Conversely, just because I entertain some feeling at this moment, I'm not necessarily going to attribute it to the character and his childhood. Conceivably the humiliation has completely disappeared—but I was reliving my childhood as I wrote *A Sort of Life*.

Have your childhood and adolescence become determining factors for you as a writer?

The Jesuits say, 'Give me a child till he's sixteen, and he's mine for life.' Everything that can happen to a person, I think, is determined in the first sixteen years of his life. The books I liked best in my childhood, those which really influenced me (I don't mean from a technical viewpoint) were not the works of Turgenev or Dostoievsky, the great discoveries of one's adult life. I loved cloak-and-dagger novels, novels of adventure, and I believe that in a way it's adventure novels I'm writing today.

My marked inclination towards melodrama stems from that adolescent reading. I've only avoided melodrama in one or two books, *The End of the Affair* and *Travels with my Aunt*. By melodrama I mean a measure of violence in the action. I must still confess to a preference for authors now rated of secondary importance, Stanley Weyman, John Buchan, Rider Haggard. I always like to pay tribute to them. When I published my *Collected Essays*, in which I devoted several chapters to them, I was in a way discharging a debt, for it was they who instilled into me this passion for writing.

You seem to have been much influenced by characters with whom you identified from when you were fourteen. I am thinking of the traitor della Scala in The Viper of Milan *by Marjorie Bowen. Here you identify not only the theme of escape, but also that of betrayal and failure; and you make a surprising statement about yourself at this time and about 'the mask of treachery' : 'It was easier for a child to escape behind his mask . . .'*

Yes, it's in the Personal Prologue to *Collected Essays.*

Does not a child escape more easily behind the mask of Zorro or of Superman, or of the heroes of the time?

I've found the passage: 'It was no good in that real world to dream that one would ever be a Sir Henry Curtis, but della Scala who at last turned from an honesty that never paid and betrayed his friends and died dishonoured and a failure even at treachery—it was easier for a child to escape behind his mask.' Of course I should have written 'this' child instead of generalizing, as I was speaking only of myself, identifying myself with the traitor della Scala.

But I did have less sinister heroes, more dazzling prospects. I suppose that Africa was one of them, because of *King Solomon's Mines.* And at last I was able to go to Africa. While up at Oxford I had even considered going into the Nigerian navy. I also thought of being a consul somewhere in the Levant. To this end I passed the stage of interviews, but I should have had to improve my French, or speak at least two foreign languages, so I abandoned the idea. I don't know where I got this ambition to become a consul in the Levant (nowadays called the Middle East); it was probably because of the English poet Flecker, who had been a consul in the Middle East. I saw myself living abroad. I even wanted to feel homesick for my native England—but all these dreams came to nothing.

I've never been a consul, not even an honorary one, and though I live abroad I'm not homesick!

Did you not tell me that you were once asked to assume a diplomatic post?

Yes. During the war. I was to be sent on an Intelligence mission. My cover would have been the post of consul in Monrovia, but the Liberians wouldn't have me, because of a book I had written, *Journey Without Maps*. All the same I nearly became a consul.

What were your other ambitions as a young man or as a little boy? Did you want to be a spy?

I had no idea of joining the secret service, if that's what you mean.

But can you mention that absurd incident when you spied for Germany in 1923?

Oh, it was just an incident in my life at Oxford. It happened during the French occupation of the Rhineland.

On the evidence, you had few scruples and little moral sense!

Nonsense! I was working in a just cause. 'Moral sense' I certainly had. I'd been reading a collection of short stories by a certain Geoffrey Moss called *Defeat*; it described the atrocious conduct of the French troops at Trier in the Palatinate, when they were trying to set up a little separatist republic in order to divide Germany. The French authorities had even installed a government consisting of German criminals whose sentences had been remitted. The Minister of Education, for instance, was an ex-convict with God knows what crime to his charge. The others had been recruited from similar sources. The French army kept the ring while the 'separatists' were busy beating up the German police. This I found scandalous. So I offered my services to the Germans; I volunteered for the role of double agent in order to find out what the Palatinate leaders were plotting, for the French had been forced to pull out. The idea of a Palatinate Republic had evaporated, but the separatists were still there, and my contact, Count Bernstorff, had told me in confidence that his friends in Berlin wanted to send me there: they were worried about the possibility of separatism flaring up again.

So my motives were quite unimpeachable. The French were trying to impose an illicit republic on the Germans— this was not Nazi Germany, but the conquered nation of 1923.

Did you already have a tendency to support the underdog?

Yes. I think I still do.

But why have you spoken of a 'double-agent'? Was it not a taste for danger which involved you in this affair?

Of course! Perhaps Oxford was pervaded by the same climate of romance and adventure that Philby and Maclean experienced at Cambridge. Andrew Boyle calls it, in his recently published book, a 'Climate of Treason'.

I used the term 'double-agent' because there was an extreme right-wing paper, *The Patriot*, owned by the Duke of Northumberland, which was supporting the French in this business of a separatist republic. So I wrote to *The Patriot* suggesting myself as their correspondent at Trier; I hoped that they would give me some letters of introduction which might enable me to glean a little information behind the enemy lines. But the Dawes Plan[1] put paid to this. I should have preferred the role of double-agent to that of spy, but I was advised that my services would not, after all, be needed. The mysterious Germans, who were such a feature of my student days, vanished as if by magic.

[1] A plan of reparations for Germany, proposed by the American General Dawes, to promote the reconstruction of Germany without ruining her economy.

I admit this was a very strange period.

My real ambition was to write, and I started very early.
My parents encouraged me—they were convinced I was
going to become a writer.

I started writing—at fourteen or even earlier—very
young, anyway. I produced bad fantasies, fables of a sort.
This propensity towards the fantastic, towards fantasy has
remained a subdued undercurrent in my work. You'll find
it in *Under the Garden*, in the short stories entitled *A Sense
of Reality*, and of course in my last novel, *Doctor Fischer of
Geneva*.

I remember the happiness, the excitement I felt when
one of these stories, *The Tick of a Clock*, appeared in the
school magazine. I sent it on to a newspaper, *The Star*,
which published it. In exchange I received an almost
miraculous cheque for five pounds. That was the first time
I earned money by my pen. I can't even remember what
the story was about. Later on I wrote sentimental fantasies
for *The Saturday Gazette*, an evening paper edited by a
woman I'd met during my psycho-analysis.

I have a vague recollection of a story in which God
quarrelled with Pan and got the worst of it. The school gave
me a prize for that one. In another story, which got me into
the *Anthology of Public Schools Verse* I had God (again)
playing a game of chess with the Devil, a game with an
indeterminate end. I wasn't a Catholic, or even a believer,
at the time.

But in spite of the cheque and the accolades for a
beginner, I was going in quite the wrong direction.

What does your first novel mean to you?

The one I wrote at Oxford? I can't remember what I
called it. I'd sent it to a new literary agent, A. D. Peters,
who later became very famous. He wrote back to say that

he'd have no trouble getting it published. Luckily he was unable to place it anywhere—I think it was a thoroughly bad book.

This failure didn't prevent my producing a second one, *The Episode*, which was no more successful in finding a publisher. I'm immensely relieved that it suffered the same fate as its predecessor. In fact I could have wished that my first three books had never been published. I'm not fond of *The Man Within*, and as for the next two, *The Name of Action* and *Rumour at Nightfall*, I'm thoroughly ashamed of them. I had to re-read them to finish the introduction to *Ways of Escape*. They're third-rate, and I wouldn't allow them to be reissued. At any rate they sold badly—which means that nowadays they're almost impossible to find.

Meanwhile I made several attempts at writing plays. One was accepted, but never reached the stage. At Oxford I also had a verse collection published, *Babbling April*. I realized then, after my first novel was rejected, that I wasn't a poet either and that I was losing my way as a writer. So in 1926 I started working for the British American Tobacco Company, hoping they'd send me to China. I had probably been influenced by Captain Gilson's *The Lost Column*, a favourite novel of my boyhood, about the Boxer rebellion. Really it was just an attempt to escape writing, a reaction. My parents, unlike most parents, approved of my vocation in the belief that all I needed was a pair of crutches—a job in journalism or some sort of employment to keep me going till I had established myself. They never actually took a hand in this, but stayed quietly in the background. Just because of their encouragement I tried now very hard not to be a writer.

The one opening I simply couldn't face was that of teaching, no doubt because of my sad experience of school, though I was fond enough of some of my teachers. There was a fair risk of falling into this trap: at Oxford my generation went into the Colonial service or the Foreign Office—or fetched up in the teaching profession. W. H. Auden became a school teacher, so did Cecil Day Lewis and Evelyn Waugh. I felt I was being pushed into teaching, which terrified me because I was convinced that once in I'd never get out again. So I decided that the business world had its attractions, and I tried to prove that I could make a success of it. I didn't want to do what everyone was expecting me to do: my spirit of contradiction was in excellent working order.

III

The Medium
and Russian Roulette

Humour and folly coexist in Graham Greene: humour to
rescue him from suicidal folly; and folly to imbue his
humour with a saving touch of informality. What place,
though, do these qualities have in this chapter? Few people
are aware of Graham Greene's gift as a medium. Even he
only takes it half seriously. And yet ...[1]

The anecdotes confided here for the first time demonstrate a thoroughly capricious side to his personality, but
one which does support his taste for bizarre jokes and his
attraction towards magic, a subject he is to discuss later on
in connexion with religion.

One might take his stories for premonitory dreams or
regard his account of the haunted house as sheer fantasy. It
is as well, though, to bear in mind that part of Graham
Greene's talent depends on his way of letting his unconscious do its work. Anything can happen, therefore. He
remains open to what others would dismiss with a sneer, so
his natural curiosity prevails over any attempt to reduce
reality to a matter of rationalization.

It was probably something in the nature of curiosity,

---

[1] As an aside, for there is no knowing whether to attribute the fact to his
magician's gift (he hates interviews, after all), or simply to the vagaries of
things mechanical, but every tape-recorder we used during our
interviews since 1975 (including the most sophisticated like the Nagra)
broke down at one point or another.

rather than any real bid for self-destruction deriving from an excessive *Weltschmerz*, which drove him as a young man to indulge in these experiments with Russian roulette. There is a disconcerting violence about them, in the pages of *A Sort of Life*.

What evidently rescued him, at least provisionally, from this self-torture was boredom, the same boredom which was later to drive him into similar scenarios of connivance with danger and death. This connivance had been symbolized on Berkhamsted Common by the revolver against the temple.

If he has been correct in saying that one has to pass through horror in order really to know oneself, then he should no longer, after what he reveals, claim ignorance of the truth about himself. Yet, after so many hours of interviews, his ignorance seems to be sincere, the paradox authentic—perhaps because in his propensity to play the conjurer, he has only skirted 'the dangerous edge of things'.

As you grew up at Berkhamsted and Oxford were there any signs of what lay in store for you?

There were the escapades and the conflicts at school which led to my psycho-analysis. Then came despair, the period of Russian roulette.

Psycho-analysis awakened in me a keen interest in dreams and the work of the unconscious. I did for a while tend to turn over stones too systematically in order to see what lay beneath them; this could have a disastrous effect on one's private life, though it can be a useful exercise for a writer, so long as he doesn't project himself directly into his novels. I realized later, for instance, that my two books

Rumour at Nightfall and *The Name of Action* were bad because I had left too little distance between them and myself. The umbilical cord was left unbroken, you might say.

My father's decision to send me to an analyst was very brave, bearing in mind how unrecognized psycho-analysis was at the time (1920). When I returned home after six months, I felt much better able to cope with school. I'd probably become a bit of a pedant, but I felt that I was considerably more 'in the know' than most of my fellows. Kenneth Richmond, my analyst, was a very strange man. He wasn't a Freudian or a Jungian but a mixture of every tendency. He relied heavily on dreams.

With the phenomenon of transfer, I of course fell in love with his wife, who happened to be very pleasant and very pretty. She's still alive, and when Norman Sherry went to visit her, she remarked, 'What a pity that Graham became a writer. He could have made such a good medium!' She said I was gifted with prescience to a remarkable degree; she based this observation on a number of nightmares I'd described to her as a child. In one of them I was by the seaside. (My dreams often have to do with the sea or water—death by drowning has been predicted for me in a horoscope.) I can still see very clearly a man stooping over the steps leading down to the interior of a ship, an enormous wave, the ship sinking. I had this dream when I was seven, in April, on the night of the *Titanic* disaster.

During my psycho-analysis, on the very night that a ship went down in the Irish Sea with its passengers and its entire orchestra, I dreamed of another shipwreck, which naturally impressed Kenneth Richmond and his wife.

A few years ago the same phenomenon re-occurred. A friend who came to see me around noon is my witness. I blurted out to her, 'Something terrible has just happened. I have an awful sense of catastrophe. I don't know if it's to do with my family.' When we turned on the one o'clock news, we heard that a 'plane had just crashed into the sea off Cap d'Antibes. There were no survivors. The passengers included an old friend of mine, General Cogny, whom I'd come to know in Indo-China in the early 'fifties.

I think there's nothing unusual in strong feelings (of fear) being picked up by other people as if they were equipped with antennae. What I have, then, isn't prescience so much as a sort of simultaneous awareness.

You have ever since your childhood recognized that you like to observe, to watch. A spy is someone who spies ... Perhaps this faculty is highly developed in you?

A very funny thing happened to me in Panama two or three years ago. Chu Chu and I (Chu Chu was one of General Torrijos's body-guards, but he also held a Ph.D. from the Sorbonne, and was a professor of mathematics—an extraordinary man, larger than life)—anyway, Chu Chu and I made many crazy excursions round the country; he stimulated my manic side. Well, outside Panama City there was a haunted house on the other side of the canal, an intriguing place. Its owner had built a bar just next door to it. The house had been unoccupied for more than forty years. The bar was called 'The Bewitched'.

We went for a drink and wanted to take a look at the house, from which (so it was said) a woman's cries were heard. The owner, an old man of eighty, would never agree to sell or let it. This had been the situation for forty years. Something had happened in that house—and it was haunted.

The windows, we found, were barred and protected by metal shutters. The doors had metal shutters too and didn't afford so much as a glimpse inside. However, by dint of walking round it we chanced upon a door with a crack in it—we could see furniture everywhere, a sort of museum.

Chu Chu was in uniform—no chance of asking to visit the house. We had to take extra precautions out of prudence and courtesy.

The owner was there every Sunday, we were told. Sunday is a feast-day in Panama. People do the round of the bars—they don't drink much except at week-ends. Anyway we turned up there the following Sunday and the bar was shut—surprising, for this should have been a 'working' day. Had the owner smelt a rat? We made several attempts, all of them unsuccessful. Later on I returned with a very pretty young woman, the wife of a Sandinista. This time the barman told us that the owner was just arriving. The young woman displayed all her charm and asked the old man if he'd show us over the house. She introduced me to him as a medium returning from a congress in Australia via Panama, who had heard about this haunted house. The old man, who was very strange, said, 'Oh, that's what they all say about a house that's been unoccupied for a number of years.' He didn't tell us, though, why he hadn't sold it or let it in forty years.

Suddenly he made up his mind to show us over some of the rooms. So, after many keys had been turned in locks, we came to a big drawing room, fully furnished; there were Victorian-style pictures of nearly naked women, china in glass cabinets. Next door to the drawing room was a bedroom. He opened the door; a bat flew out.[1] There was an iron bedstead in the room, with bedclothes in a disorderly heap.

I felt sure that forty years ago the old man had murdered his mistress and then claimed that the house was haunted to explain the cries and to prevent the house being searched. (I had mentioned the house to Torrijos, who had

---

[1] Graham Greene is terrified of birds and bats.

known of it since his childhood. I suggested that he send soldiers to break in under cover of a military exercise. 'But that's illegal!' he had said. 'We must act within the law.') Anyway, the old man pointed to the floor and asked me, 'Can you guess what's under there?' I didn't have the nerve to reply, 'A woman's skeleton.'

When we left, I had the notion of giving him a Masonic handshake on parting, so instead of shaking his hand in the normal way, I exerted a slight twist on his fingers. 'Ah,' he exclaimed; 'you're a medium *inconscientemente*. I am a medium *conscientemente*!' As my Spanish is very poor I understood him to mean that I was a rather immoral medium while he was a moral one. But that was not it: what he meant was that he had the faculty of recalling what he had 'seen' as a medium, which he claimed to be, while I was a medium who, on coming out of a trance, simply forgot. And he added, 'I could show you a great many other things, for it was here that the Spaniards hid their treasures. We're on the gold route, between Portobelo and Panama City, where the slaves who had hidden their booty were killed and buried by the Conquistadors. I could tell a tale of hauntings . . .'

I never saw the old man again.

Even so, you are haunted by the Other in yourself.
Yes. Psycho-analysis didn't free me from him.
But why the Russian roulette at nineteen?
A death-wish, I suppose; a sense of dissatisfaction with myself. I remember myself as an adolescent, not knowing who or what I was. I would look in the mirror and think, 'What in heaven's name am I?'

I had found the revolver in my brother Raymond's drawer. I knew straightaway how I would use it. During the Revolution Russian officers, I had read somewhere, used this sort of drug: the moment the finger depresses the trigger, the surge of adrenalin through the system has the effect of dissipating boredom. Those few months when I practised Russian roulette I don't think I really wanted to die. It was simply a game with an element of risk; it enabled one to appreciate what one had risked—life itself. It was not suicide. The chamber could take six bullets; I would insert only one, so I gave myself each time five chances of survival out of six. Proper suicide requires a great deal more courage. In periods of deep depression, throughout my life, I've often wished for death—but I've always lacked the resolution.

Some of your characters commit suicide; is that not suicide by proxy?

I think that most people have, at one time or another, thought of this solution.

And you, have you often done so?

No, not often, but sometimes. For some while now the temptation to suicide has become less forceful. The last occasion was when I took a glassful of aspirin, like the man in *Doctor Fischer*, in a tumbler of whisky. That was about thirty years ago. I'd been reading a crime novel by Dorothy Sayers, in which a murder is committed by an old school friend. He gets his crony drunk in a night-club and then challenges him to toss back a half-pint of whisky all at one go—what was known at Oxford as 'a sconce'. As he'd already drunk a great deal, the result of this was to kill him—from a heart attack. So I told myself that this time, to ensure that I didn't survive, I'd add some two dozen aspirin to the glass of alcohol. But the effect of the whisky was offset by the medicine and I slept very well that night.

Why did you try to commit suicide?

It was during one of my bouts of depression. Boredom, which has always brought on my neurosis, lies behind my experiments with Russian roulette. I discovered then that I was manic-depressive—I needed a flick of the whip to keep me going.

Paradoxically it was boredom which put an end to the game. I grew tired of Russian roulette as of everything else. The terror of the moment gradually dissolved. I had the same feeling during the London Blitz. One felt fear for an hour or two, then one grew tired of it and fear, especially if the air-raid was prolonged, turned to boredom. One had quite simply reconciled oneself to not surviving. One said to oneself, 'This is the end, so whether it comes in half an hour or in two hours ...' It's the hope of survival that generates anguish, for anguish lies in the conflict between the hope of surviving and the fear of not surviving.

Well, one day I disappeared onto the Common for my usual game of Russian roulette. I pressed the trigger once. Nothing. I reloaded. A second time. Nothing. Then I put the revolver back in the drawer once and for all—I had become indifferent to my own death.

IV

Writing and Action

Free to move as he pleased and yet riddled with inner conflicts, Graham Greene left for an unexplored part of Africa in 1934, asserting that he had an imperative need for travel and action. Even though he modestly claims to have always had a return ticket in his pocket, his adventures give occasion for surprise or even dismay, and laughter too, for he enjoyed the absurd. Gravity takes turns with buffoonery, depending on whether he is in Haiti or in Panama, whether he is quietly doing the rounds of the night-clubs in Batista's Havana or tasting the horror of war, trapped between the Viet-minh and the French paratroops.

Narratives such as *Journey Without Maps* and *The Lawless Roads*, which trace his adventures in Liberia, then in Mexico, reveal the temperament of a dedicated explorer, one who can endure a high degree of discomfort. During our strolls by the waterside at Antibes he would speak offhandedly of the 'ticks on my backside' acquired during his travels on mule-back in Tabasco in 1938, or again of his recent mishaps in Belfast, a place worse than Al Capone's Chicago. He announced, furthermore, that in future he was going to tread carefully because, he said with a laugh, he had reached 'the age when things go snap'.

One does not believe him, for one knows that he is just back from Nicaragua where he has been to assess the progress of his friends the Sandinistas. Last year he even declared that 'he would have been ready to enlist' at the side of General Torrijos if the General had been unable to reach an agreement with the Americans on ratifying the Panama Canal Treaty.

It must therefore be recognized that the constant sense of humour which affords him a measure of objectivity does in fact conceal a redoubtable observer, a forceful and courageous reporter. Few people have his gift for 'sensing' a country. When he expresses his love of Africa, his words are all the more moving in that one can gauge how deep his roots have gone. Graham Greene is a man of attachments. The subject of Panama and the friends he made there induce him for once into a talkative mood. Regrettably he only indulges in anecdotes if he believes that this will serve to evade questions about his own life.

His endless travels around the globe could encourage a suspicion that he is rather a dilettante; but when one hears him talk, with statistics to hand, about the very tangible preoccupations of the Nicaraguans faced with the consequences of Reagan's election, one realizes soon enough that the journalist in him is truly at grips with reality, and that this man, who could meet Ho Chi Minh in the middle of the Indo-China war, who had contacts with Castro's guerrillas and with the Sandinistas before the fall of Somoza—he clearly must know a great deal more about world affairs than his self-inflicted isolation at Antibes would lead one to suppose.

It is difficult and pointless to dissociate his travels from his books. As he explains further on, certain novels do without a background while others apparently need one. On the other hand his missions in Malaya and among the Kikuyu, for all their dangerous and unusual character, furnished material only for articles which were to be a prominent feature of his book of memoirs. Why these exceptions, why was there no link between action and writing? Graham Greene's reply is evasive: no book came out of these experiences, for no particular reason.

Had he perhaps, just for once, escaped from writing? For, let there be no mistake, Graham Greene the journalist, the 'explorer', the adventurer, never disarms Graham Greene the writer: he remains too much attached to his obsessions. In the last resort, as it emerges from these dialogues, action is important only in so far as it has an outlet in writing. Could the writer dispense with action? Is it action which leads him to write? The problem is falsely stated: for Graham Greene, writing is a form of action. This is what makes his universe coincide with the hard realities which he exploits.

This urge to take risks, like a continuation of the Russian roulette, has constantly driven you into the forefront of danger, from Indo-China to Liberia, from Haiti to Malaya, in the very 'heart of darkness'. Have your travels and your news stories given you some respite from boredom? Have they succeeded in recovering for you the fear concealed in the Russian roulette and your childhood despair?

Death is not something I'd willingly go searching for today. In 1978 I went to Belfast, but I only stayed there five days. I fled this climate of fear, it was too oppressive. Danger interests me less than it used to, so I'd no longer find the courage to play at Russian roulette—not willingly, at any rate. But when one has no choice ... I'm thinking of a mishap which befell me in 1967 near the Suez Canal, soon after the Six Day war. There I was, flat on my face behind a sand dune, under Egyptian fire. I felt frightened to begin

with, then bored, then irritated. It was simply going on too
long—two in the afternoon till five ...!

Were you not 'simply' courageous?

No, it wasn't a question of courage. I've already told
you, panic can only last a moment. Fear is different: one
grows accustomed to it, which becomes terribly boring.
I've experienced panic twice in my life, as far as I can
remember. The first time was in London when the police
baton-charged the crowd at a Mosley demonstration. It
was a little before the war. With police protection, Mosley
had organized a provocative procession of his black-shirts
through the East End with its strongly Jewish population.
There was a counter-demonstration. I went along to
watch; I wanted to see what would happen. The crowd
panicked and tried to escape from the batons. I really did
panic then, by contagion, I suppose.

The second occasion when I remember panicking was
during one of my visits to Indo-China; I found myself for a
few minutes lost and isolated between the French paratroops and the Viet-minh, during the fighting around Phat
Diem in North Vietnam. I dared not move. The paratroops
were behind me, the Viet-minh in front, hidden in the
bush. I didn't fear death so much as being wounded. I said
to myself, 'How stupid it would be to lose a leg or to be hit
by shrapnel for no reason at all, in this country which is not
mine, in a war which is none of my business.' But it was
only a fleeting terror.

What a modest reckoning for a whole lifetime of adventure!

I don't know if I'd call it an adventurous life. Danger
doesn't attract me as much as it used to, because its
counterpart, boredom, becomes more benign with age.

*What was it that sent you recently hurrying to Panama and
has kept you in a state of alert?*

Curiosity ... curiosity ...

Not some sort of dilettantism!

I should not have returned so often to Indo-China if I'd been a dilettante. If a country interests me I like to study it in depth. I want to be as close as possible to the action. Since you've mentioned Panama, I remember that Torrijos on one occasion wanted me to be present at the exchange of hostages captured by the Sandinistas when they took the National Palace at Managua in August 1978. I was to be on board the 'plane leaving Panama to pick up the political prisoners released by Somoza in exchange for the members of parliament and other notables held in the palace by the Sandinista guerrillas. I was in no danger. Panama was neutral, even if it supported the Sandinistas. But at least I would be a little nearer the action. Torrijos, who became one of my best friends, warned me the previous evening via Chu Chu. Torrijos had given instructions to Chu Chu that we must be ready to take the 'plane for Managua between four and five a.m. But Chu Chu was drunk that night, and failed to grasp the whole of his chief's message. Torrijos had in fact advised us to spend the night at the airport, for no one could tell precisely when the 'plane would take off. When we reached the airport at four a.m. the 'plane had already left half an hour before, much to my disappointment.

That does not explain why and how you happened to be in Panama in such a privileged situation.

General Torrijos, whom I didn't know at the time, first invited me to visit his country four years previously. And just as I fell in love with Indo-China on my first visit, so I fell in love with Panama and its people, just like that, without warning. After that the General invited me every year. In 1974 the negotiations for the signing of the Canal Treaty looked as though they would drag on for a long time, with possibly no agreement at the end. Perhaps

Torrijos knew that I was inclined to take an anti-American attitude and was glad to have a well-disposed observer on hand. We soon became close friends.

I also grew extremely fond of Chu Chu, the man appointed to act as my guide. He was a remarkable person, formerly a professor of Marxist philosophy in the University of Panama under the last presidency of Arnulfo Arias. When Torrijos and another colonel seized power and set up a military junta in 1968, Chu Chu thought it wise to leave Panama and go to the Sorbonne to study philosophy. He soon learned that the other colonel, a Rightist, had been put on a 'plane to Miami by his ex-ally Torrijos. (For them Miami symbolized the city of ditched politicians. The entire Arias clan lived there, with all their money.) When Chu Chu realized that Torrijos was Left-inclined he returned home. Torrijos, however, was not a Marxist, so Chu Chu was given no leisure to teach Marxist philosophy; he became a professor of mathematics as well as a security guard. He even wrote a little book called *The Theory of the Insinite*. I asked him what this 'theory of the insinite' was all about. 'Well you see,' he said, 'I lost one of my front teeth, and when I taught I often caught myself pronouncing the word infinite as insinite!'

We'd go for long drives around the country which I grew to love more and more. This was a period of great happiness; my boredom was left far behind. Each visit gave me occasion for amusement. Torrijos himself had a highly-developed sense of humour. During our excursions Chu Chu would talk about his various women and his marital problems; he would recite Rilke in German at the wheel and I'd have to try matching him with quotations from English poets.

Those five years in Panama certainly relaxed me, but also brought with them a political commitment in a number of

(57)

ways. I felt involved in the ratification of the Canal Treaty. I was fascinated to see such a little country holding its own against the Americans. When Torrijos invited me to join the Panamanian delegation to Washington I found it amusing—and of course it was an honour too—and when I disembarked at the military airbase with the Marines all presenting arms, the national anthems blaring, the red carpet, it gave me no little pleasure to recall that for years I hadn't been able to set foot on American soil without a great to-do because of my supposed membership of the Communist party at nineteen. Here I was coming back on an official Panamanian passport. Torrijos too saw my little intrusion on American soil as a splendid joke.

Had you felt the same kind of jubilation on your previous visits to Latin America—to Havana, for example?

I wouldn't speak of 'jubilation' where Havana's concerned: Cuba wasn't a happy country under Batista.

All the same, paradoxically, what you derived from an event as serious as the Cuban revolution was an entertainment, Our Man in Havana *in 1958. How do you explain that?*

In the introduction to the book I wrote that originally, just after the war, I had a film in mind. My friend, Alberto Cavalcanti, asked me for a screenplay, and I wrote the outline of a story making fun of the Secret Service. The story was to be set in Estonia before the war and concerned the recruitment of a somewhat unorthodox agent by the English. The film never saw the light of day because the censors did not appreciate the notion of poking fun at the Secret Service. I realized subsequently that it wasn't easy to make a joke out of a person like my hero, who had perhaps indirectly helped Hitler. So when I came to write the novel I moved the scene from Estonia to Cuba, which I had known well enough in Batista's day.

Havana before Fidel came to power in 1959 was a bizarre, corrupt city with its brothels, cheap drugs, gambling saloons, all owned by Las Vegas. Everyone went there for a good time. It was only in the mountains, where Castro's rebels were already gathering, that the situation was serious.

Are you not sorry you wrote an 'entertainment' instead of a book like The Quiet American, *which would have carried more weight?*

Not in the least. I think that *Our Man in Havana* is a good comic novel. The object was not to talk about Cuba but to make fun of the Secret Service. Havana was merely the background, an accident—it had nothing to do with my sympathy for Fidel.

What attracted you to Cuba?

In Batista's day I liked the idea that one could obtain anything at will, whether drugs, women or goats. One day I asked a taxi-driver to get some cocaine. He was back in a few minutes with the powder he'd bought at the street-corner. When my friend and I went to our room to inhale it, I said to her, 'This isn't cocaine, it's boric acid in powder form, I'm sure of it.' Havana was a place for comedy rather than for drama.

I made trips around the island in 1957 and stayed there in 1958. In April 1959, after the revolution, I was back there to help Carol Reed make *Our Man in Havana*. Later, in 1966, I managed to meet Fidel at a little house outside Havana. Do you see that picture above my sofa? He gave it to me. I later discovered that he had told a mutual friend, Carlos Franqui, who introduced us, that if he liked me he would offer me the picture, otherwise he wouldn't. After a three-hour conversation he took me into the kitchen; on the table lay this canvas painted by a Cuban artist, Porto-Carrero. He asked me, 'Do you want it? May I make you a present of it?' And on the back of the frame he wrote his greetings.

At the time of the revolution I felt very close to the Fidelistas' struggle. I brought them a large suitcase full of winter clothes—if it was very hot at Santiago, in the surrounding mountains the nights were freezing and they couldn't obtain suitable clothing. Customs barriers had been set up in the lowlands, especially around Santiago, Batista's headquarters, at the foot of the Sierra Maestra. If one took the 'plane from Havana to Santiago one had to go through Customs there at the airport as though one had come from a foreign country. A Cuban carrying warm clothing to this hot tropical city would necessarily have been suspected of taking them into the Sierra Maestra, while *I* could always say I was on my way to visit my daughter in Canada. So I carried two suitcases, mine and the other, a bulky one destined for the guerrillas. Another way in which I could help—in London I had a friendly Labour MP always ready to ask embarrassing questions about the British government and the Batista regime. Cuba had become, as you can see, one of my commitments.

During my visits there, six in all between 1957 and 1966, I met several heroes of the revolution and a few survivors of Moncada. There was Fidel, and also Haydée Santamaria, the wife of Armando Hart, a young lawyer who became Minister of Education and now is, I believe, Minister of Culture. I contacted them when they were in hiding in a house in Santiago. Armando Hart was in the process of having his hair dyed by a Fidelista hairdresser. He had just escaped from prison in Havana and was preparing to make for the Sierra Maestra. Haydée Santamaria's fiancé had been tortured, then murdered by the police after the attack on the barracks at Moncada. Batista's police had dragged Haydée to the prison to show her his mutilated body with its eyes torn out. She was an admirable woman, a brave and good woman, a heroine of the resistance. I've just been saddened to learn that she has committed suicide, though not for political reasons. I was also able to meet Raul Castro's wife, Vilma Espin, who was very active in Fidel's cause. I met, too, Fidel's friend Carlos Franqui, who was planning to ghost Castro's autobiography. He lives in Rome, now, where he has written a very good book on the war in the Sierra Maestra. A story which amused me was about the beautiful Vilma Espin. She was hiding in a house at the foot of the Sierra Maestra. Suddenly the police burst in while she was in bed. She leapt out of the window into her neighbour's garden, all white in her nightdress. Her neighbours fell to their knees and started praying—they believed they had seen the Virgin Mary descending.

The travels you have just described efface the image of a neurotic and encourage the idea of a man who knows how to enjoy himself, even when he is afraid. You complained one day, though, that you have devoted yourself to your writer's profession to the detriment of living. Have you not written and profited from living?

I didn't 'complain'. One sometimes writes sentences which are taken much too seriously or literally by the reader, when all the author has done has been to exaggerate a little in order to emphasize his message. What you're alluding to is an idea expressed in particular circumstances: V. S. Pritchett, Elizabeth Bowen and I had been asked to broadcast about works which had influenced us. I was sure that Pritchett would write that he had been strongly influenced by Chekhov and Turgenev, Elizabeth Bowen by Henry James ... so I deliberately restored the balance by announcing that the books which had most influenced me at the outset were those of Marjorie Bowen, Rider

Haggard, Stanley Weyman. I went on to add that after reading *The Viper of Milan* by Marjorie Bowen I had found myself trapped into literature. Her novel had supplied me with my pattern in the carpet—which religion was to explain for me later. I was in a way being provocative. Just as on another occasion, in January 1948, François Mauriac and I had to take part in a conference in Brussels on the question 'Is Christian civilization in danger?' As I knew that Mauriac was going to say that the Russians could reach Paris in a week and that Christianity was in danger, I decided to announce that Christianity was not in danger. So I chose to develop a parable of the last Pope turning up in New York or London, a wretched, hunted figure with no baggage except for a shabby cardboard suitcase, who, as he was executed as the last Christian, transferred his belief to his executioner, and thus Christianity survived.

But what do you really think? Have you written and got the best out of life?

I have to the extent that life has furnished me with subjects for my writing.

We are going round in circles!

Yes, we're going round in circles. Leave aside the pleasures of food, wine, sex, all which is summed up in 'getting the best out of life'—and what's left? (I expect that food and wine also have a bearing on what one writes . . .) But doesn't getting the best out of life mean enjoying a certain experience? I've made the most of this experience in my writing.

There is inevitably an interaction between experience and writing. My articles on Indo-China from 1951 to '55 resulted in *The Quiet American*, even though I had no intention of turning them into a book, not even after my second visit for *Paris-Match*. It was a sheer accident, in fact, that took me to Indo-China the first time. I had just

(62)

spent three months in Malaya in 1951 as special correspondent for *Life*, to cover the guerrilla war known at the time as the Emergency. An old friend of mine, Trevor Wilson, who had worked in the same department as me during the war, was now Consul General in Hanoi, so I thought it would be a good idea to look him up on my way home from Malaya. I spent only two weeks in Indo-China, during which time I saw my friend and met Marshal de Lattre. I was immediately fascinated by the country and by what was going on there. In Europe very little was known about the situation. The English press had only a single correspondent covering the whole of Indo-China and he was a Reuter's man; the stories in the English papers were filed in Paris for the most part. American journalists were thin on the ground; very little was known about this French war.

It wasn't till 1954 that I realized that a novel had taken hold of me and that I would have to return a fourth time to Indo-China: I didn't yet have enough background to accomplish my task.

On the other hand *A Burnt-Out Case* resulted from quite a different set of circumstances to those behind *The Quiet American*. In this case it was the novel itself which had set me in motion. So I went to the Congo in 1959, to the leper colony at Yonda, in search of a character and a plot, as I explained in my diary of the journey.

Were you not suspected of leprophilia? What a bizarre subject it must have been, this Conradian experience of horror!

I had prepared myself for the worst. As a rule I am very distressed by illness or infirmity. In the Congo I certainly expected to be horrified, but the day I arrived, Michel Lechat, the doctor of the leper colony, knew exactly how to handle me. The first time I accompanied him to the dispensary, which was out in the open, he handed me a little bottle of ether and said, 'If you feel a bit awkward (his English was not very good), if you feel a bit awkward, breathe some.' And he told me about a Belgian government minister who had passed out on a visit to the leper hospital. So I said to myself, 'I can do better than that minister, can't I?' As a result I never needed his ether bottle.

The visible signs of the disease were not very shocking. The boy who looked after me, for instance, had lost all his toes, but he had special shoes to walk in. I was surprised at how little I was affected by the sight of these infirmities. I should add that I seldom felt embarrassed in the presence of a leper. I think, anyway, that in *A Burnt-Out Case* I don't overdo the leprosy which is not, after all, what the novel's about so much as about what goes on in the minds of the characters. This book marked a turning-point in my work, and in it I think I succeeded, as I told you, in breaking the pattern in the carpet.

This was far from being the case with *The Honorary Consul*. It was the plot itself which took me to Argentina in 1969 while I was at work on *Travels with my Aunt*. I had seen the town of Corrientes (the scene of *The Honorary Consul*) by chance from the river-boat taking me from Buenos Aires to Asuncion in Paraguay when I was working on *Travels with my Aunt*. Something in the atmosphere of this town struck my imagination—I don't know what it was. There was nothing to see, just a little harbour and a few houses, and yet a sort of surreptitious charm was already at work. There's an old saying locally that once you discover Corrientes you keep going back. I was unaware of this saying at the time, but, so far as I was concerned, it proved true. When I wanted to write the story of a man accidentally kidnapped by guerrillas I calculated that the Tupamaros or the Montaneros were much too experienced to make such a mistake. If the novel was to be plausible, they

(64)

had to be Paraguayans sufficiently cowed by Stroessner's dictatorship to be still inexperienced. Then I remembered Corrientes, on the Paraguay/Argentine frontier, and decided to return there in search of a more authentic background.

Are you in fact capable of working without background, without an exotic element?

I think so. Is any country less susceptible to inspiration than Switzerland, which I chose as background for my last book? It would be wrong to imagine that my novels are always set in exotic places. *The Human Factor*, *The End of the Affair*, *A Gun for Sale*, *It's a Battlefield*, *The Confidential Agent*, *Brighton Rock* are all set in England. On the other hand I've gone for news stories to countries far more exotic than Cuba or even Haiti, but no book took shape out of my experiences. I'm thinking especially of my visit to Malaya during the Emergency, or my travels in Kenya during the Mau Mau uprising.

I'm surprised when readers ask me why I've chosen this or that subject as though it were the author who made the choice, whereas it's often the subject which chooses the author. There are times in fact when I'm inclined to think that our entire planet gravitates inside a fog-belt of melodrama. I've expressed the idea in *The Ministry of Fear*. The protagonist, Rowe, in an air-raid shelter during a raid over London, imagines a conversation with his mother and addresses her as follows (if you'll permit me to return to this passage):

'This isn't real life any more,' he said. 'Tea on the lawn, evensong, croquet, the old ladies calling, the gentle unmalicious gossip, the gardener trundling the wheelbarrow full of leaves and grass. People write about it as if it still went on; lady novelists describe it over and over again in books of the month, but it's not there any more.

'I'm hiding underground, and up above the Germans are methodically smashing London to bits all round me. You remember St Clement's—the bells of St Clement's. They've smashed that—St James's, Piccadilly, the Burlington Arcade, Garland's Hotel, where we stayed for the pantomime, Maples and John Lewis. It sounds like a thriller, doesn't it, but the thrillers are like life—more like life than you are, this lawn, your sandwiches, that pine. You used to laugh at the books Miss Savage read—about spies, and murders, and violence, and wild motor-car chases, but dear, that's real life: it's what we've all made of the world since you died. I am your little Arthur who wouldn't hurt a beetle and I'm a murderer too. The world has been remade by William Le Queux.'

And yet when the coincidences or paradoxes of reality come too close to fiction, does that deprive you of your material as a writer?

Not necessarily, but it can happen. One can meet a person in the flesh who seems to have been set in one's path just in order to have a book written about him. After four years in Chu Chu's company I found him as entertaining and interesting as ever. But the idea of a novel about him came to nothing—Chu Chu was his own novel. There was no extracting a book out of him. He was an adopted child, not one whom I'd carried in the belly for nine months. Now the whisky priest in *The Power and the Glory*, (his original took up only a couple of lines in *The Lawless Roads*, the journal of my travels in Mexico), was not a man I met, he emerged from some part of me, from the depths.

So it is not the spectacular, dangerous or ludicrous aspect of these travels that matters, but what goes on inside you. What made you go in 1934 to Liberia and Sierra Leone?

In those days young writers made that sort of rather

dangerous journey. Perhaps it was a way of proving oneself. Peter Fleming had his *Brazilian Adventure*: he went off in search of a Colonel Fawcett who had vanished somewhere in the Amazon basin. Evelyn Waugh made a difficult trip round British Guiana which forms a chapter in one of his novels. As for me, I was certainly trying to escape tedium, and that was a good way for a young writer to set about it. I had no experience of travel in Africa and the expedition soon turned out to be foolhardy. There were as yet no up-to-date detailed maps of Liberia. All I could lay hands on was an American military map; it showed whole areas left blank except for the word 'cannibals', and dotted lines took the place of rivers. It wasn't an easy journey and I imagined I would never feel any wish to revisit Africa. Of course, when the Second World War broke out and the Secret Service needed someone with experience of this continent, I found myself volunteering for Liberia. But the Liberian government wouldn't have me, as I'd published a travel book on their country, so I had to knock at Sierra Leone's door. After I'd been there a year I fell in love with the place.

What is it like, this love of Africa?

I love the smell of Africa—West Africa. I feel nothing like the same attraction for East Africa, still less for North Africa. It's a sort of magic. I like the Africans, the beauty of the scenery and the women. Freetown is a charming old town with a most lovely bay. After the war I returned twice to Sierra Leone, then went to the Congo and to Kenya, but these other countries never appealed to me as much. I think the attraction of West Africa has something to do with the nature of colonization. The whites in Kenya are farmers, owners of land, often arrogant, while the white population in West Africa consists mostly of traders and colonial officials. No white man was allowed to own land in British

West Africa; the land belonged to the Africans. It was the tribal chiefs who made the laws, which meant that the atmosphere was quite different from the one created by the white farmers in Kenya.

My travels in Sierra Leone and Liberia in 1934 lasted altogether three months. I'd set out on the venture with no experience other than the reading of books by various explorers of West Africa, books by Livingstone and by Mungo Park, a great eighteenth-century traveller whom I particularly admired and who had gone up the Gambia and the Niger. My head was full of *King Solomon's Mines*, which I've mentioned to you, and of the adventures of John Buchan's *Prester John*. As an adolescent I identified myself with the heroes of these novels. I suppose this is what drove me to cross Liberia and enter areas where no white man had been seen before.

So my passion for Africa, which was quite subjective and emotional to begin with, crystallized in the course of an adventure which I undertook partly to write a travel book. This was the only way I could afford such an experience, for I was very poor at the time. My publisher had given me a three-hundred-pound advance for *Journey Without Maps*. Unfortunately the book was withdrawn from sale because I'd quite inadvertently given one of the characters I met the name of a government doctor in Freetown. I didn't know this doctor, who was not in Sierra Leone when I was there, but he threatened to take me and the publishers to court if the book was not withdrawn. It was a blow for me: I'd already spent my advance, which put me further in my publisher's debt. The book was only reprinted many years later.

What is striking about your travel writings is your concern to go as close as possible to the front line, both in human and in geographical terms. During your reportage *in Kikuyu country, during the Mau Mau terror, you complain: 'In Indo-China, even in Malaya, there was something approaching a front line ... Here ... I was still far from the real stage ...' Why this impatience, this attraction towards 'the dangerous edge of things'?*

Because I want to go deeper, to be more implicated. I'm constantly saying to myself, 'How am I going to describe this? How can I ensure that the reader will see what I'm seeing?' This preoccupation is all that enables one to endure some grisly sights.

As a young man I had so little tolerance for the description of accidents that I'd have to stoop down and pretend to tie my shoe-laces, otherwise I'd faint—my imagination carrying me well beyond the actual description. In London before the beginning of the Blitz I was still quite nervous for the same reason. I joined an air-raid warden's training course, but I was not at all sure I'd be able to cope with a bad accident. When the bombing came, though, I was no longer a mere spectator, I had a job to do, I was active, and no longer afraid of my emotions.

The sight of other people suffering may perhaps relieve your own personal suffering?

I don't think that has anything to do with it. When one is a rescue worker, or a reporter, or indeed a writer trying to bring a scene (however ghastly) to life, one is active, and this activity enables one to bear the weight of suffering.

How does your journalist's instinct harmonize with your writer's instinct?

Let me say that I've never been a professional journalist. When I was working for *The Times*, from '26 to '30, I was a subeditor and not a reporter. It was only when I became better known as a writer that I could get myself despatched to places that interested me—Indo-China, Malaya, Kenya. I expect that the amateur journalist is closer to the writer than is the professional journalist, because he's entirely free in his movements and opinions.

My journalistic experience as such has been of little consequence, but it has helped, I think, to increase my European readership compared with that of some other English authors. I've travelled a great deal, and have been interested in a wide variety of events and situations. The French appreciated *The Quiet American* and the Spaniards have been drawn to me with novels like *The Honorary Consul* set in Latin America.

But there's one great distinction between the writer and the professional journalist: a written or televised *reportage* is only read or seen once, after which it disappears into the archives, while a novel carries on for a number of years. My first book, *The Man Within*, which is still in print today, was first published fifty-two years ago.

Why have you so often chosen as background poverty-stricken countries, countries crushed by war or dictatorship, like Haiti and Paraguay?

I had made several visits to Haiti, but always quite by chance, as a tourist. When Papa Doc seized power I wanted to see what had changed, for many people I knew there were at risk. I had one friend in particular whom I greatly admired. He was a physician and philosopher, and he was Minister of Health in Paul Eugène Magloire's government; he later had to resign. He was the direct inspiration behind Dr Magiot, the Communist in *The Comedians*, though my friend, who often attended philosophy congresses in Europe, was never a Marxist. When I returned to Haiti in 1963 for *The Sunday Telegraph*, he had fled. He has since died in New York. Other friends, writers, priests whom I knew less well but still wanted to see again, they too had disappeared.

To come back to the question of why I choose this sort of country, I think it's because the experience confronts me with a rather curious phenomenon; in places which are stricken if not by poverty at least by distress (Poland in 1955 was not a 'poor' country), it is paradoxically easier to make friends. People are more willing to talk, intimacy grows rapidly, and the worse the distress, the more quickly one finds out.

Is this distress not a necessity for you?

Possibly; I wouldn't know. Could I be attracted by what I hate? Anyway, if you think about it, name me a novelist who has *not* described suffering. It's an integral part of life. Aside from P. G. Wodehouse, for whom I have an enormous respect, and whose novels are inspired by an infectious *joie de vivre*, do you know many novelists who write about happiness?

But why do you inflict this grey anguish on your characters and on your readers? Horror always lurks in the background.

Not always. Not in *Our Man in Havana*, *Travels with my Aunt*, even in *The Confidential Agent* the ending was fairly happy, wouldn't you say?

Yes, you are right. But it is such a provisional happiness, and it comes after so much anguish.

I don't know if I torture my readers. All I am aware of is putting ideas down on paper. I suppose those which occur to me are sometimes sad, but I don't think I carry horror to the extreme you imply—except of course with Pinkie in *Brighton Rock*. Pinkie is a monster. Horror is there in this novel; one can set a finger on it. Where my other books are concerned, I don't think there's any question of 'horror'. I'd rather call it sadness, a sadness from which one emerges. Aristotle has an expression for the sense of relief which follows sadness—catharsis. All tragedy brings with it this sort of relief. In *The Human Factor* one is relieved of the weight of sadness because the two characters, Sarah and Maurice, love each other. It's because they love each other that one is sad at their separation, but it's also a relief to know that their love continues to exist. If she had betrayed him while he was in Moscow, or if he had betrayed her, then one might speak of horror.

And what about Querry taking refuge among the lepers? And the body in the swimming-pool, in Haiti? And Pyle, the quiet American, coolly wiping his shoes spattered with the blood of his victims?

I've told you there was nothing horrific in the sight of leprosy. The corpse in the swimming-pool was my invention, I never saw it, any more than I saw Pyle after the bomb attack. These pictures symbolize the horror of the war in Indo-China and of Papa Doc's regime. Some scenes are in fact based on actual facts like the theft of the coffin by the Tontons Macoutes in *The Comedians*.

It's true that I have had to witness some scenes of horror in the course of my travels. Why? Because I'm interested in politics, so that I'm interested in places where things are happening. And in places where things are happening one can't avoid running into some degree of horror—not an abstract or metaphysical horror; an objective, political horror.

V

The False Political Disloyalties

'Political horror': weaker mortals turn away from a man who dares look it in the face. To see it is to reveal it and to become a leper who rings his bell of warning as he approaches. This is why the American government mistrusted him for a long time, to the point of refusing him a visa. This is why Papa Doc was beside himself with fury when *The Comedians* was published; he felt unable to resort to physical violence, so he paid his stooges to put out a pamphlet denouncing Graham Greene as 'a pervert', 'a man unhinged', who 'assuages his sadistic instincts'. The introduction to the document is reproduced overleaf; should one laugh or weep on reading it? Graham Greene claims that it constitutes one of his greatest sources of pride.

The author seldom looks back with any shudder after his intrusions into the 'deadly' zones of politics. If Haiti made such a deep impression on him that it haunted his dreams, a more common experience was to laugh up his sleeve at the thought of the irritation he was causing. Many of Graham Greene's hatreds—and friendships—are instigated, for he is a provocateur. However, as he does not write novels to prove any thesis, the majority of his readers probably fail to perceive the danger he can represent and the complexity of his political commitments. The popular stereotypes, crucifix, revolver and trilby still tend to prevail.

Yet one would do well not to take Graham Greene on trust but to step beyond the rather simplistic signposts indicating him as a 'writer converted to Catholicism in 1927', or 'member of the Communist party for four weeks in 1923'. One would do better to watch out for what he has called 'divided loyalties': these are revealed, in his books and in his life, as seeds of revolution, sown all the more deceptively in that they do not correspond to any logic but his own.

He is not to be found where one expects him, and of course he turns up where one does not expect him. If one comes upon him in flesh and blood among the Latin-American guerrillas, one is surprised later on to find him unsympathetic towards the Provisional IRA. He makes a sharp distinction between guerrilla and terrorist. It is no doubt for that reason he has not been heard supporting the Palestinian cause even though he has quite a few reservations about Begin's present government. He is fascinated by the Communists, those believers constantly on the edge of losing their faith, but he appears to be deeply disappointed at not having been able to find 'Communism with a human face'. Yet, oddly, he does not condemn the invasion of Afghanistan as vehemently as that of Czechoslovakia.

These examples of paradox are endless, for the explanation of his political vision of the world—if vision it is—and of his impressive hold on the world rests on the very variety of his options, and indeed derives from this variety. One then realizes that this restlessness, this sort of instability and incoherence, these paradoxes in which he and his characters tend to evolve (the sacrilegious priest in his grace, the spy in his betrayal, the writer in his unscrupulousness) form a whole. This entity is still too constricting a concept for Graham Greene, who told us five years ago that he did not think there was the slightest coherence in his political vision; the entity borders on anarchy. Graham Greene is an anarchist of international class; a dissident in perpetual schism with settled societies. He is motivated in his work by the 'virtue of disloyalty' presented almost in the form of a manifesto in 1969 at the University of Hamburg, where he clearly stated that the storyteller's task is 'to act as the devil's advocate, to elicit sympathy and a measure of understanding for those who lie outside the boundaries of State approval'.

'Of any State', one should add, for his vision clearly transcends the British parish-pump mentality which he goes on to deride; it is a global vision, it probes the abyss. What carries conviction in his work is its depth—a depth descending (in *The Third Man*) into the sewers. His starting point is his own isolation as an individual; his action may be overt and official as in his letters to the press, or discreet in the tangible help he brings to revolutionary movements. When he speaks one is struck both by his violence and by his restraint. He gives full vent to his anti-Americanism, for instance, but he remains conscious that his position places on him a sort of duty of reticence, and this duty he obeys to the letter. Much remains in shadow: the meeting with Ho Chi Minh, his reticence in judging Castro, etc.; yet one could swear that, in spite of his provocative utterances, this 'devil's advocate', this devotee of mystery and ambiguity has no skeleton in the cupboard. What he draws on is a spirit of rebellion which may often seem questionable simply because we are behind the times, or he is ahead of them.

While his 'clairvoyance' is striking, however, what is most impressive of all is the genuine strength of his

(75)

sympathies. Behind his subtleties, behind his aversions (which are merely the counterpart of his preferences), behind his attraction for the horrific, he betrays in his writing and actions the anarchic 'human factor'. It is the human factor which overrides the dichotomies; it makes one of his characters say, 'If I love or hate, let me love or hate as an individual ... I wouldn't kill for Capitalism or Communism or Social-democracy or the Welfare State.' He can turn cowardice into bravery, failure into nobility, claptrap into a moving statement once he has reached 'the dangerous edge where belief wavers'. It is the human factor which Greene hunts like some rare game.

Introduction to 'Graham Greene démasqué finally exposed'
(Pamphlet published by the Haiti Department of Foreign Affairs. Lucien Montas was Head of Cultural Affairs in this Department. The other signatories were the Haiti Minister of Information, the Foreign Minister, etc.)

Graham Greene reveals himself, after all, as he is, as he always has been—a queer character riddled with a thousand complexes and obsessions. He lives out a veritable inner drama, and he uses literature, which should be for him, as for others, the ideal means towards sublimation, as a way of inflicting on the weak—or on those he takes to be weak—the nightmare fancies of his delirious indignation and this pessimistic vision of the world, the creation of a thoroughly perverted and unbalanced ego.

The hideous face of poverty, the dubious charms of vice, the wounds of exploitation and injustice, these are what he delights in. But one has to have the means to assuage one's passions. Greene is, therefore, the ideal instrument, the more so as his talent permits him to broach the most equivocal subjects while laying claim to a pleasing veil of respectability, or of art. He often writes to order.

(76)

With *The Comedians* he achieves a double coup: he assuages his sadistic instincts, gives himself leisure to exercise his negrophobia and at the same time rounds out his bank account by serving, luckily without success— superfluity in all things is harmful—those who would denigrate the world's First Black Republic, regarded by some as decidedly a bad example, especially under the leadership of Dr François Duvalier who means to inspire the Haitian with pride about his origins and who pursues, with success and determination, the battle for the economic and cultural independence of the Haitian nation.

A proud, a dignified black man has to be humbled at all costs and, if possible, eliminated. Called in to meet this challenge, Graham Greene finds the game all too easy, for the task is admirably suited to his innate tendencies. But he applies the paint a little too thickly, he smears the whole painting, his tired old techniques are all too obvious.

It has been easy therefore to dismantle the pieces of his 'Infernal Machine' one by one. That is what we are going to do, and it will be seen clearly enough that the accuser has no moral authority, no authority of any kind, to fulfil his role and carry out his task of demolition.

On the one hand we have an unbalanced man, a pervert, a writer with a pessimistic vision writing to commission. On the other hand we have a little coloured nation which has written in its blood the most glorious pages in the history of the emancipation of peoples, which intends to live free and independent, forging its destiny with admirable tenacity and courage, in suffering and incomprehension. How could one have thought it possible to set the one against the other . . .?   LUCIEN MONTAS

(77)

A rather silly journalist has claimed that I've spent my life building hell with my novels after failing to locate it in the course of my travels. There seems to me to be enough drama in reality without making literature the sole depository of hell—which I persistently refuse to believe in.

What I *am* quite ready to believe is that fiction and our unconscious are permeated with reality in all its horror. Even our dreams are encrusted with it. I was haunted by Haiti for years after my last visit. In these nightmares I'd be there incognito and have to escape somehow or other before I was discovered.

Did these nightmares relate to any concrete experience? Were you directly threatened?

Papa Doc and his Tonton Macoutes managed to turn the country into a particularly macabre place. But I did feel personally threatened after the publication of *The Comedians*, in which I described some of the grim realities of Haiti. Duvalier took the trouble to answer back: he had a hostile pamphlet published in English and French; it was written by people who've become ministers under Bébé Doc, and claimed to prove that I was a 'drug-addict', an 'agent of an imperialist power', the 'shame of proud and noble England', etc. Even today people arriving in Haiti have their copy of *The Comedians* confiscated if it is found in their luggage.

I felt very ill at ease on my last visit. My every move was watched. 1963 was a very bad year, one of the blackest, for in the north of the country a small guerrilla group was operating—I was able to meet the members a year later. A few rebels were also at large in the south. I wasn't allowed to visit the north. I was constantly being searched for arms.

In what circumstances were you able to meet the guerrillas in the north?

Their group had managed to cross the frontier and take

(78)

refuge in the Dominican Republic. As I needed to complete some notes for *The Comedians*, I made a trip in 1964, not to Haiti itself, but along the Dominican-Haitian border. It was in San Domingo that I met one of the group leaders, Fred Baptiste, who became a friend of mine; so did his brother Raynald (who played the part of a Tonton Macoute in the film version of *The Comedians*). The Dominican government had allowed them to set up their headquarters in an old lunatic asylum, just as in the novel. Later, Fred Baptiste and his brother returned to Haiti to fight. They were captured and died in prison. Haiti has not changed much—I still receive a lot of information from exiles. Three years ago, there was reason to hope for a slight relaxation in the reign of terror, but Bébé Doc changed his mind and the Tonton Macoutes are as virulent as ever. Of course they never really disappeared: they were rechristened 'the leopards' or 'the panthers'. The grisly woman, who ruled the prison at Fort Dimanche, is back at her post, as powerful as ever.

Did you come across her in person?

No, but I knew of her existence because of my friends tortured in prison. I was shocked one day at finding nothing but travel articles in the American papers describing the splendours of Haiti and the life in its luxury hotels, with no mention of the actual conditions in the country, the poverty, the oppression, and I thought it was high time to induce the American press to print something of the truth. The International Journalists' Club in London invited me to a lunch where there would be a session of question and answer. This time I seized the opportunity to say what I knew about repression in Haiti, and I threw a challenge at Bébé Doc: I told the press that I'd be only too glad to return to Haiti and take note of every change for the better, but on one condition—that my friends Fred and Raynald

Baptiste met me at the airport. I'd learnt that Fred had gone mad in prison, and that his brother's condition was grave. And I thought: if they go ahead and kill them now because of my declaration, at least they'll be free of their sufferings.

The American papers relayed my message. The Haitian government responded with an article in one of their daily papers, renewing their attack on me. This was shortly after the death of Papa Doc, in 1971.[1]

The Comedians is the only one of my books which I began with the intention of expressing a point of view and in order to fight—to fight the horror of Papa Doc's dictatorship.

Otherwise you do not believe in the power of a political literature?

Certain books have clearly enough exercised a considerable political influence, but mine don't belong in this category. I don't as a rule write to defend an idea. I'm content to tell a story and to create characters. In an article one can try to express a direct point of view, but not in a book. I don't want to use literature for political ends, nor for religious ends. Even if my novels happen incidentally to be political books, they're no more written to provoke changes than my so-called 'Catholic' novels are written to convert anyone.

And yet one has the impression that you often try to combat injustice, especially in The Honorary Consul *and* The Quiet American.

---

[1] On 7 July 1969 Graham Greene had written to *The Times*, accusing its editor of having published a photograph of Governor Rockefeller presenting a letter of congratulation from President Nixon to this 'murderer and executioner', President Duvalier. Graham Greene said that while the contents of the letter were not known, all those who had heroically risked their lives in an attempt to overthrow Papa Doc were bound to see the letter as an endorsement of tyranny.

In *The Honorary Consul* I was not fighting anything or anyone in particular. It was the characters and their ideas, or rather the evolution of their ideas, which interested me. As for *The Quiet American*, my animosity against American policy in Vietnam certainly gave it its fundamental tone, but it can't be said that I was attacking the American presence—their involvement in the country at the time was too slight to justify my doing so, and I couldn't attack a hypothetical future. In fact I don't fight injustice: I express a sense of injustice, for my aim is not to change things but to give them expression.

Are you not being evasive when you refuse to admit to certain responsibilities? Are you going to be like Simone de Beauvoir who, when asked how she saw her role of 'militant', answered that she was 'above all a writer', that she was 'only a witness', that she would never, for instance, have 'thrown a stone in May 1968'?

Oh I'd throw a stone without hesitation! I'm not talking about May '68. (I'm not French and was in Italy at the time.) I still want to take an active part in change. I've been a modest help to the Sandinistas in buying bullets which, I hoped, would eventually hit Somoza. That's the same as throwing a stone, isn't it? But you see in such a case it isn't the writer who is involved—it's a character called Graham Greene who happens to be a writer.

'Even an opinion is a kind of action,' explains Fowler, the reporter in The Quiet American. *I suppose that for you writing is after all a sort of political act. Is that enough?*

It sometimes happens that a writer can make a sharper impact with his books than if he signed petitions and tracts. Writing is certainly a kind of action. But Fowler also says that he is not a correspondent: 'I preferred the title of reporter,' meaning that he merely wrote down what he saw, he was not 'committed'. In a *reportage* events have to be described as vividly and accurately as possible. It was on this basis that I tried to describe the siege of Phat Diem. From the journalistic viewpoint, I was faithful to the notion of respecting the truth. I may, of course, have made mistakes—I can think of one or two—but they were 'honest' mistakes resulting from wrong information.

A reporter mustn't on any account set out with preconceived ideas or give his allegiance to the paper which employs him, otherwise he fails to see the faults, be it of the French or of the Viet-Minh.

In this case you rely entirely on your own judgement?

Absolutely: but I am scrupulous about checking my facts.

In contrast with writing books, you proceed on a basis of facts, which is relatively solid in spite of the physical risks, would you not agree?

There are far more and far subtler risks for a writer. To go to write a news story is something of a holiday for me; a novelist is a creature without scruples, which is tiring. The novelist's station is on the ambiguous borderline between the just and the unjust, between doubt and clarity. But he has to be unscrupulous, as I've already remarked, and I've been misunderstood. I would take Mauriac as an example not to follow. I'm a great admirer of some of his books. But his loyalty to the Catholic Church has made him rather too 'scrupulous' a writer—in the theological rather than in the moral sense. I expressed this idea in the lecture at Hamburg. A writer must be able to cross over, to 'change sides at the drop of a hat. He stands for the victims and the victims change.' This obliges him to violate his faith or his political opinions, to be unscrupulous, but it's indispensable.

But how far can this disloyalty go?

I don't know. I've never tried to reach the end.

Do you always think, then, that 'to choose one's side is to render oneself insensitive to the infinite complexity of human situations, to limit one's understanding of the world, to limit one's own freedom'?

That's true up to a point. Sometimes it's impossible not to choose one's side, as in the last war against Hitler. I think that when I wrote the passage you quote I must have been thinking of socialist realism, for which I have no sympathy. What I was offering was an opinion on a specific question.

You have just taken two extreme examples, Hitler and Stalinism. Between the two there are none the less infinite possibilities of choice to which one must submit in spite of everything 'if one wants to remain human' as Fowler says. Sometimes you do not really take sides but you remain human. How do you do it?

Don't I always take sides in the end?

When, though? You often fish in troubled waters. You are attracted by a certain sort of Communism but you do not choose it. The 'heretics' Küng and Schillebeeckx interest you, but you do not support them.

Because instead of taking one side or the other I take both, rather than making no choice at all.

What, then, are you? Both a writer 'free not to take sides' and a dispassionate reporter, bound by your professional conscience?

A little of both, I think. I'm not entirely Fowler.

In your books you seem to want to maintain at all costs a sort of balance between what in abstract you consider just and your own sympathies which pull you in extreme or contradictory directions.

That's just about it . . .

But is it difficult?

It's a matter of how one masters emotions which can surface too readily. I try to write coolly. This means that I restrain myself a little, I detach myself from my emotions

(83)

at the moment of writing. At the moment of feeling, I expect I'm as emotional as the next man.

Do you not feel guilty of political inaction?

Not in the least. For me political action is writing and nothing else. I've helped and defended some people by my writing, I've attacked some people by my writing. For instance I did what I could when Daniel and Sinyavsky were sent to prison. I asked the Russians to stop translating my books. I also tried to arrange for my blocked royalties to be remitted to their wives—but here I met a blank wall. There was not a chance. That wasn't the first time I expressed my opinions as a writer. I resigned from the American Institute of Arts and Letters to make a stand against the war in Vietnam, and I tried to carry certain foreign authors with me, though they didn't follow my lead. I've also written some open letters—not many. One I wrote was to Malraux in *Le Monde* of 23 June 1960, to protest against torture in Algeria. I quoted a passage in one of his books, *Les noyers de l' Altenburg*, where he said, 'The individual is unimportant. But then an unexpected thing happens; everything changes, the simplest things, the streets for example, the dogs . . .': and I asked him how he, after writing such a beautiful sentence, could still belong to a government which was responsible for torture in Algeria. I also wrote to the Archbishop of Paris, who had forbidden prayers at the grave of Colette, at her funeral—though here it was more a question of morals than of politics.

You reckon, then, that a writer can have a political or moral weight. Do you think, like one of the characters in The Comedians, *that 'A pen, as well as a silver bullet, can draw blood'?*

It's a pleasure when a dictator like Duvalier reacts; it proves that he's been hit. I certainly upset General Stroessner with an article on Paraguay and with passages

(84)

from *Travels with my Aunt*. During an official reception in Washington before the signing of the Canal Treaty, attended by dictators like Videla and Pinochet, a moment came when I stood near Stroessner of Paraguay, a particularly formidable character. A Panamanian woman who was with me grabbed hold of another member of Stroessner's entourage, and said, 'This is one of General Stroessner's ministers ... allow me to introduce ...' The man held out his hand. '... Mr Graham Greene,' the woman continued. The extended hand dropped at once. The man almost spat in my face. 'You once visited Paraguay,' he said. Then he turned on his heel and went to join his chief. I thought to myself. 'Ah well, at least I've left my mark on him!'

In relatively 'civilized' countries one's 'fame' is a protection. I would run no danger in a Communist country, even though I know that they could take advantage of the fact that I'm not unknown in order to bring pressure on people I might have met there. But in Haiti, when I was allowed to visit the south of the island, I said to myself, 'This would be an excellent opportunity for Duvalier to get rid of me and blame it on the guerrillas.' Similarly, in 1979, when the Sandinista guerrillas asked me to join them as an observer, I refused: Somoza could have had me shot down and put the blame on my friends, which would have given him an excellent propaganda point— 'Graham Greene assassinated by the Sandinistas ...' When I was younger and less well-known, thirty or forty years ago, I was less protected, but my presence was no doubt less of an embarrassment to those I was in contact with.

Similarly as a measure of prudence I've always refused to carry a gun in zones of armed conflict. In Kenya during the Mau Mau uprising, and in Malaya, if I had walked into an ambush, the rebels would simply have picked up

(85)

another weapon. I remember in Kenya giving a lift in a hired car to a chief's son, whose first question was whether I was armed. I told him I wasn't and he exclaimed, 'I see that you trust in divine providence!' In Indo-China, on the other hand, I felt rather ashamed at being without a rifle, one afternoon when I found myself alongside some French paratroopers at the siege of Phat Diem. I was given one to sleep with that night, in case we were attacked—but I wouldn't have known how to use it. Back in England I told myself that I ought to be a little more familiar with handling weapons, and I spent a day at a barracks learning about the Bren gun, just in case. Luckily I never had occasion to use one.

What do you think of a man like Régis Debray and what happened to him in Bolivia? He too had been invited to Managua, particularly to celebrate the revolution. He was even seen parading in combat uniform with the guerrillas in the streets of the capital. The Sandinistas had shoved a submachine gun into his hands.

I'm rather in two minds over Debray, though I admire his books. I'm afraid that he never in fact grasped the nature of his responsibilities. I found it a little disappointing that he should have worn a uniform (especially as it's well known that the Sandinistas didn't have many—most of them came from the Panama National Guard).

Would you not say that this was a mark of respect for the Sandinistas?

This is only my personal opinion, but if I'd allowed myself to wear a Sandinista uniform—which is barely conceivable given my loathing of uniforms—I'd have felt not that I was paying them respect but that I was appropriating a share of their glory. As for carrying a rifle when the fighting's all over, it's like a disguise—I hate disguises.

Are you not a little severe towards a man who probably 'went to the limit of his loyalty'?

Quite probably, because I for my part very seldom commit myself a hundred per cent. I'd be too afraid of being labelled a 'political author' (which happens now and then), just as I've been labelled a 'Catholic writer', because I don't think that my way of writing or my attitude to writing has been in the least determined by events. Events have merely had an occasional influence on my choice of subject. I suppose I can be called a political writer when I tackle political subjects; but politics are in the air we breathe, like the presence or absence of a God.

You told me one day, à propos of religion, that you kept 'a foot in the door'. How big is the foot that you keep in the door politically speaking?

Perhaps the foot I keep in that door is even bigger, though I fear this may be due to gout.

Oh dear, where does that leave us? ... You have recently claimed that you are less concerned with politics because you recognize that you have become 'less masochistic with age'; but on the other hand I have the impression that for some time now you have been anxious to emphasize the element of commitment in your work.

My remark about masochism was just a joke. Besides, my interest in politics goes back a long way. Don't go thinking, as many others have done, that I've undergone some evolution from religion towards politics. The first three books I wrote were just straight novels, and the fourth, *Stamboul Train*, was a thriller with only faint political overtones. But my first overtly 'political' novel, *It's a Battlefield*, was written in 1935, before *Brighton Rock* and *The Power and the Glory*. *The Confidential Agent*, published in 1939, also points to political preoccupations. For some years now there's been a preponderance of novels with a political flavour, but religion still interests me as much as ever.

I don't know what is meant by a 'committed' writer. I refuse to belong to this party or that. Take Churchill: he began as a Liberal, then he opted for the Conservatives; he changed his party. Disloyalty is inherent in politics. But whatever I've said about disloyalty, I hold to certain ideas, and there I haven't changed. I know that people are supposed to grow reactionary with age, especially those who were the most revolutionary at the outset. This is not true of me: I have always inclined to the Left, ever since my first books, and my sympathies have consolidated with age. There's a certain coherence, a certain continuity between *It's a Battlefield*, *Brighton Rock* and *The Honorary Consul*: it's my concern with the possibility of social change. The effect of poverty on Pinkie and Rose in Nelson Place makes *Brighton Rock* a social novel as much as a so-called 'Catholic' one. I'm sometimes accused of being a reactionary. Someone even wrote that he saw me as a Conservative—and practically a Fascist—Catholic. George Orwell defended me in a letter of his; he said he thought I might well belong to a species which was new, and possibly even unknown, to England: that of the Catholic 'fellow-traveller'. An exaggeration of course.

For a long time the Catholic image had been identified with a Conservative one. Catholicism was associated with Franco, when in fact even in Spain the Catholic Church stayed neutral during the Civil War. The Dominicans were neutral, and the Archbishop of Seville was a vigorous opponent of Franco. I don't know why it was then assumed—perhaps it still is—that Catholics support Right-wing dictatorships. But I've come across Left-wing dictatorships who've interested me a great deal more!

Because they were, I suppose, little lost dictators?

Do you call Ho Chi Minh a little dictator? And Fidel, do you think he can be considered a 'little' dictator?

Of course not, but I did not imagine you would consider them simply as 'dictators'.

I wish that the word 'dictator' didn't necessarily imply a pejorative. Let's say that Castro is certainly an authoritarian statesman. As for Ho Chi Minh . . .

Let me take this rather underhand opportunity to ask you in what circumstances you met Ho Chi Minh. What you say in your Essays does not explain the motives behind this 'mission' to him in 1955.

I'm not free to talk about it. All I can say is that I was asked to hand him a letter. The 'mission' was carefully prepared. I even had to resort to a touch of blackmail because it was difficult to get into Hanoi once the French had pulled out. Of course I was interested to meet him and I was able to verify a certain number of small details. For example a rumour was circulating among the French, at the time I met him, that he was no longer in charge: he was of course a wonderful old man, but now served only as a figure-head. I was able to dispose of this rumour at once: when I arrived at his house in Hanoi, I was received first of all by the Minister of Information, who gave me to understand that he spoke no French. Of course I spoke no Vietnamese. He didn't know English either. He brought me to the drawing-room where Ho Chi Minh was waiting for me. Ho Chi Minh spoke fluent English. The three of us took tea together. As soon as Ho Chi Minh had left us, his minister rediscovered his French. He had no doubt been afraid to say a word to me before he had checked whether I was in Ho Chi Minh's good books. This behaviour seemed to me totally at variance with the role of figure-head which was being ascribed to Ho Chi Minh.

When did you become politically aware?

I think that in the 'thirties one couldn't help being aware of what was going on, much more so than in the 'fifties and 'sixties or perhaps even during this last decade. One felt war quite obviously looming in Germany with the sinister prospects taking shape there. In England there were hunger marches, thousands of people were out of work. Fascism appeared with Mosley. When the blackshirts paraded, the police were there—to protect them. They tended to lay into the counter-demonstrators, which boded no good. You can find this atmosphere in *It's a Battlefield*.

Yes, but I do not see why you consider it to be a political book. You denounce in it injustice, the humiliation of the poor, in an aggressive enough way, certainly, but does that not reflect a humanitarian rather than a political stance?

It seems clear enough to me that the book is political to the extent that, even if I don't adopt the Communist viewpoint (in fact I poke gentle fun at a cell meeting and at a Communist intellectual, Mr Surrogate, a Communist writer but a well-heeled one), I do attack the government head-on. The book came out at the time of violent demonstrations in Hyde Park, in which some policemen were hurt. It tells the story of a man who, to prevent a policeman from clubbing his wife, hits him too hard and kills him. The man is thrown into prison. The death penalty still existed in those days, so the man risked his life. I denounce all this in detail in the novel. Isn't that taking sides? V. S. Pritchett certainly thought so: he considered that the novel was practically a sociological treatise— London poverty in the 'thirties.

But even so, one of your reactions of the time has troubled me, when I read A Sort of Life. *I mean your activity as a strike-breaker during your period on* The Times *as a sub-editor, during the General Strike. It seems to me that in that particular case you were more on the side of the Conservatives, were you not? You ought to clarify this point.*

You're quite right. At that moment I was emotionally attached to the newspaper. The strikers had set the building on fire in order to put an end to the paper. As a member of the staff I was on the defensive. And in fact out of curiosity—I think it was essentially a question of curiosity—I went on patrol with the police at Vauxhall for two or three days. But you know, the story was more complicated than it seemed. Not only did *The Times* have to fight the strikers, it also had to fight off Churchill, who was trying to launch his own paper with the support of the extreme Right; if *The Times* had foundered, it would have dragged down all the rest of the moderate press. I don't regret my attitude at the time—I was very young, twenty-four.

But have you not regretted what you seem to consider a youthful prank, your membership of the Communist party?

Oh that! I was even younger then, nineteen or twenty. It was a joke. Two of us were in it together, Claud Cockburn and I. He did, incidentally, become a Communist, a genuine one, and a very good writer. During the Spanish Civil War he served as a special envoy to the Republicans under an assumed name. He's written a very good autobiography and three excellent novels.

We got ourselves party cards, the two of us, because we had some idea of a little trip to Moscow all expenses paid. That was in 1922-3, only five years after the Russian Revolution, with Lenin still alive. Very few Oxford men had joined the party, so we thought we'd make the most of it and take charge of the cell. But eventually someone who was sharper than we were tumbled to our frivolity so we didn't press the point and we left. Claud Cockburn worked on *The Times* when I did and was soon appointed *Times* correspondent in Washington, an important posting for a journalist. He subsequently let the whole thing drop, for he'd become a real Communist—he *was* genuine.

And, for better or for worse, this story of your membership of the Communist party has dogged you all your life.

It was my own fault: it all started when the McCarran Act was passed, around 1952, in the United States. I was in Brussels, where I met the First Secretary at the American Embassy. He told me that the State Department was against the McCarran Act and was trying to scuttle it by coming up with cases to demonstrate its absurdity. For instance there was the famous Italian conductor Toscanini who had been banned from the United States on account of this Act. So I said to him, 'If I revealed my murky past, would that help?' 'It sure would,' he replied. So when *Time* planned what they call a cover article after the publication of *The Heart of the Matter* and sent a journalist to interview me, I showed him my Communist party card which I'd kept in a drawer, with four sixpenny stamps to prove that I'd paid my dues four times in four weeks. Strangely enough this card carried a number: 1. I don't know how this could have happened because at Oxford there were already ten other members. The journalist made a scrupulous report of the facts, repeating word for word what I had said. So I inevitably fell victim to the McCarran Act. For years afterwards, each time I wanted to visit the States I had to obtain special permission from Washington, give them notice of my arrivals and departures, give detailed flight information and so on. My visits were restricted to three weeks. I can't say that I was really banned from the country, but these permits took time, and the red tape often proved a nuisance.

One day I had to be in New York to receive some Catholic prize for *The End of the Affair*; as I was on my way back from a *reportage* in Indo-China I thought I'd take the occasion to stop off in Hollywood, where a film director was turning the book into a film (a very poor one). So I chose to reach New York only a few hours before my three-week visa expired. There, before a highly respectable audience, in a highly respectable Catholic university, I made a very short speech: 'I can only say a few words to you for my time is limited. The Attorney-General of the United States requires me to leave tomorrow morning. Good-bye.'

These vexations lasted till Kennedy's election. He had sent an excellent ambassador to London, David Bruce, who gave a lunch in honour of those of us who had been elected honorary members of the American Academy of Arts and Letters. The year was 1961. The party included Elizabeth Bowen, Henry Moore, Charles Snow, and myself. As I was sitting next to the ambassador I told him how strange it seemed to be receiving this honour while I couldn't even obtain an ordinary visa for the United States. Two weeks later they telephoned me with the news that an open visa was awaiting me at the embassy. I made use of it at once to go to Cuba, stopping off in New York, to show them that, so far as I was concerned, nothing was going to change!

Your loyalties are not all that divided with regard to the Americans!

No. The temptation to double allegiance tends to disappear before American capitalism and imperialism. I would go to almost any length to put my feeble twig in the spokes of American foreign policy. I admit this may appear simplistic, but that's how it is. Some time ago there was an article in *The Spectator* about *The Quiet American*, which said that it made little difference whether I inclined to the Right or the Left, since what I truly detested was American liberalism. That wasn't far wrong.

I did indulge the notion that things might change if Carter were re-elected. The idea of a return of the

Kennedys horrified me—but Reagan's election was the worst thing that could have happened.

You are a Westerner, an Anglo-Saxon. Do you not think that your aggressive attitude towards the Americans comes from your famous spirit of contradiction?

No, this sort of revulsion goes back a long way. You can find traces of anti-Americanism in film reviews I wrote in the 'thirties, though I did have a great deal of good to say about certain Hollywood productions, but my animosity doesn't derive from the cinema. It goes back to my first visit to the United States, between 1937 and 1938. That winter I travelled about a great deal before going to Mexico to look into the religious persecution there. I have always felt very ill at ease in the States, except in San Francisco, a much more European city than New York. The terrifying weight of this consumer society oppresses me.

You made a remark to a Times *reporter which could shock many people: 'If I were given the choice between the United States and the Soviet Union, I'd choose the Soviet Union.'*

That's not what I said. Besides, it was an ironic remark. I said I'd rather 'end my days' in Russia than in the United States. I was alluding to the fact that, as a writer, I might end my days in a concentration camp—if I was important enough for that. In the United States, on the other hand, the writer counts for nothing: he's not regarded as influential. In Russia at least they pay attention to him: he's an interesting citizen, even if his days are numbered.

Russian materialism is less solidly anchored than American materialism. In the USSR there's more of a latent sense of religion however deeply buried. Perhaps that's the reason why I have felt a sort of attraction for Communism. I've noticed for example that criticisms of my books made by Catholics or Communists have a

(94)

dimension not to be found among others. They succeed in disclosing more. I don't know how to define this supplementary perception. I've an impression that they have a better understanding of what a writer intends.

I don't know, either, how to explain my attraction towards Communism. Deep down, one has always nurtured this dream, perhaps a naïve one, of Communism with a human face, and this regret that the Tsarist traditions have proved too strong to be effaced by the revolution. If Marxism had established itself in a less backward country, perhaps world Communism today would look very different. One begins to despair of Communism with a human face. When I went to meet Allende in 1971, I told him straightaway that he must be wondering what I was doing in Chile. And I explained it was 'because I'm forever searching for this Communism with a human face.' Allende was not a Communist; he was a Marxist, but his government included members of the Chilean Communist Party. But after witnessing Allende's fall, or Dubček's— though Allende's was brought about by America and Dubček's by the Soviet Union—one concludes that Communism is unlikely ever to escape from Stalinism or dictatorship.

You are attracted by Communism but apparently not by Communist countries. None of them, except in the last chapters of The Human Factor, *have served as backgrounds for your novels.*

I don't really like China at all. When I stopped in Moscow on my way back from a trip to China, I almost had the feeling of a return home, of being back in Europe. Contacts were so much easier to make in Moscow. One could let one's hair down over a few glasses, while in China—it was during Mao's Campaign of the Hundred Flowers—one sensed, behind the polite smiles, a perfect indifference. It was impossible to engage in any real discussion—there was simply no response, only a great politeness, a total void. In Russia I made friends. I paid four visits to Moscow. I took my son there to celebrate his twenty-first birthday. I think my visit in 1961 will prove to be my last, for I came down with a bad attack of pneumonia. That's why in *The Human Factor* certain details from scenes in Moscow are a little dated.

Can you tell us about the circumstances of your visit to Prague in 1969? What was your role?

Dubček was still in office, but I didn't meet him. I'd gone to Prague at the invitation of the Writers' Union and of Josef Skvorecky (who now lives in Canada), to protest against the Russian troops' invasion of Czechoslovakia ... When I arrived, Skvorecky had left the country twenty-four hours earlier, but I had the pleasure of meeting Smrkovsky—he was one of the three ministers who had been dragged off to Moscow—and I found him very likeable. I saw him at breakfast, and I asked him what he thought of Kosygin who, in our Westerners' eyes, seemed marginally more sympathetic than Brezhnev. He told me that when the three Czech prisoners were called in to a joint meeting with their three Russian counterparts, Brezhnev, Suslov and Kosygin, there was nothing in the Russians' behaviour by which to tell them apart: the same gestures, the same words, the same style. But he thought he detected in Suslov's eyes a hint of understanding, which is interesting, for Suslov was in a way the party theologian and, as a Leninist, he may conceivably have felt a secret distaste for the invasion of Czechoslovakia.

Where were you when you made your protest speech?

At Bratislava. I told them ironically that I had had the honour to find myself in their country twenty-one years earlier, at the precise moment of their revolution: 'Bliss was it in that dawn to be alive' (you know the words uttered by Wordsworth at the time of the French Revolution). I told them I was there in February 1948. But what had become of this revolution? What was left of it? That's how I began, in front of two or three hundred people in a hall hired by the Czech Writers' Union. Husak still held the post of First Secretary of the Slovak Communist Party (he was to become First Secretary of the Czech Communist Party in April 1969). The table was littered with microphones, and I started my speech in such a way as to see how many people in the hall understood English. 'I hate a lot of microphones on the table. They don't bother me when they're under the table or hidden in the ceiling ...' Laughter broke out all over the hall, so I could conclude that most of them knew English. The speech, of course, was a powerless demonstration, but my visit to Czechoslovakia enabled me to make contact with writers like Havel and Milan Kundera, whom I greatly respect: a respect, mark you, which has nothing to do with our various political opinions—I never read a book for the political opinions it expresses.

Once again you found yourself in a country at a critical moment in its history, but not, in this case, accidentally. Your presence had a political significance. What was the significance of your presence in Prague during the 'revolution' of February 1948?

I was there quite by accident. I was in Vienna doing some research for the screenplay of *The Third Man*, before going on to Rome to meet a woman-friend, to work on it for four weeks. To fly from Vienna to Rome at that time, one had to go by way of Prague. I had two publishers there, so I took the opportunity to look them up. I could not foresee that I'd arrive just in time for the 'revolution'. The Viennese papers made no mention of it. I was surprised to find two English journalists on the flight, being sent to Prague 'just in case'; one worked for the Associated Press, the other for the BBC. We arrived late at night: a snowstorm had caused problems with our landing. In Prague it was impossible to find a room, so I slept on a sofa in the room which the two special correspondents had been prudent enough to reserve. This gave me the chance of a close look at how the professionals 'covered' a revolution, and I found it very funny. (Before that, I'd nearly always travelled alone, except in 1934–5 in Africa, when my cousin was with me. Afterwards in Malaya, Indo–China, Kenya and elsewhere I preferred to be on my own so as to avoid being hampered by the viewpoint of other journalists.)

As we had been given no supper on the 'plane, we asked for food when we reached the hotel, but there was none. All the porter could suggest was that we go down to the basement where the staff were holding a ball. There we fell in with all sorts of people. The ball was in full swing. The Venezuelan ambassador, and others too, had realized that food, drink and entertainment were to be had for a song. He danced with the cook, and we danced with whoever came to hand. It really was, on the surface, a successful and happy revolution.

In the morning I went out to take a turn in the streets. The two journalists got up late and telephoned their local correspondents to enquire if anything was happening. They were told 'no', and went back to bed. I went out for another walk and in a side street was approached by a man who had been following me. He told me that he wanted to go to the British embassy, that he was a scientist, that he'd invented a guided parachute: it could land the parachutist fifty kilometres from where he had jumped. This seemed to me perfectly plausible. He whispered, 'Now that the

Communists have arrived, my invention will fall into the hands of the Russians. Will you help me and go to your embassy and tell them?' I had the idea of asking him if he had any other patent to protect. He told me that he had invented a machine to build a wall at the rate of thirty centimetres a second. So I didn't go to the embassy.

You have sometimes been charged with naïvety, especially by John Le Carré, your colleague in espionage.

I don't know what experience—if any—John Le Carré can have had of the secret service. He is much younger than I, and his political experience seems to me consequently more restricted than mine. You are alluding to a radio interview in which he said that I was much too simple, not to say naïve, to be intruding into the field of politics[1], and that I hadn't progressed beyond the problems of the 'thirties, when the action was being played out in a fairly schematic manner between Communism and Catholicism. It's very naïve to imagine that the problem no longer exists in these terms. It may be true that enforced atheism is an absurd relic imposed by nineteenth-century Communism which confused philosophy with economics; but it would be dangerous to ignore the persecutions still being perpetrated on religion. The confrontation between Communism and Catholicism is still very powerful.

I'm very much aware of this problem, for I went to Poland in 1955, soon after Stalin's death; and even twenty-five years ago the confrontation was as serious as any in the 'thirties. Cardinal Wyszynski had been placed under house-arrest. It was the time of the 'Pax' movement, which was more than a little dubious; the Communists were seeking a way to infiltrate the Church and set up a 'Polish National Catholic Church'. It is absurd to say that this

[1] BBC radio interviews produced by Philip French, op.cit. p. 24.

problem concerned only the 'thirties. You only have to look at what's going on in Poland today, for instance . . . [1]

What strikes your readers is not your naïvety or obsolescence, a charge from which you have just defended yourself, so much as your far-sightedness. How do you explain this clairvoyance of yours: your choice of the missile crisis in Our Man in Havana *(1958), your detecting the role the Americans were to play in Vietnam after 1955, or the political kidnappings in South America in* The Honorary Consul *(1973)?*

It seems to me that too much has been made of this so-called faculty. My story of concealed missiles in Cuba was a sheer fluke. In the case of *The Quiet American*, it was very easy for someone who had spent four winters in Indo-China to grasp the situation in which the Americans were going to be enmeshed. One could put a finger on a number of operations set in hand by the CIA (the CIA was behind the bomb attack in the Saigon square which I mentioned in the novel, for example). But that did not represent war, and I can't say that I predicted it; I was content to suggest the American undercurrents in the French war. It's not a question of foresight but of ground reconnaissance. Every good journalist should be able to recognize the signs of the times. As for political kidnapping in South America, that didn't begin with my honorary consul.

Even so, you often happen upon revolutions 'by accident': there was Prague in 1948, revolutions in the making, like Cuba and Nicaragua, or you land in battle zones. You say you went to Malaya because your brother was there, and to Indo-China 'by chance, to see a friend in Hanoï'. It was an accident that A Burnt-Out Case, *which is set in the Congo, was 'conceived'*

[1] This interview took place in November 1979.

*during the Léopoldville riots in 1959. Are we to believe such a
succession of coincidences? Are you not sometimes taken for a
sort of walking detonator?*

The instances you've mentioned really were a question
of chance. I wouldn't pretend to be a walking detonator,
even if I've provoked the anger of some right-wing
dictators.

*It is difficult to accept your answer about chance. Yesterday
you were telling me of the problems encountered by Torrijos
over the ratification of the Canal Treaty. You mentioned that
if the Americans had refused to sign, something would have
happened. So you were already acquainted with the possibility
of a conflict, you were a step ahead of ordinary people. You
were, in a way, on the inside.*

If I was a step ahead of the European Press, it was
because I knew Panama and was a friend of Torrijos. There
was really no secret. The Americans were fully aware of the
situation. Their chiefs of staff had said that a hundred
thousand men would have to be deployed along the canal
to prevent sabotage.

I don't believe that my friendship with some men in
power, or my encounters with people like Ho Chi Minh,
Allende, Castro or Paul VI have helped me to a deeper
knowledge of what is going on. I met them because they
interested me, that's all. I could in passing, pick up a few
scraps of information, but that's not 'clairvoyance'. Chance
always plays its part. I was not anticipating the riots in the
Congo, I was looking for a character for purely personal
reasons. I heard almost nothing about the riots as I spent
practically my whole time in a leper colony, which I left
only to visit other leper colonies. I did realize that the
Belgians at Coquilhatville were terrified. The local governor slept with a revolver under his pillow and called the
police every time he heard footsteps near his house at night.

But the priests were very calm. For once, the nature of my preoccupations had drawn me a long way from the conflicts in the news. Mine was an inner journey. This is no doubt why *A Burnt-Out Case* represents a breaking away from my other books.

Perhaps clairvoyance may enter into *The Human Factor*, only the future will tell. I prefer to call it common sense. This has to do with an imaginary threat which menaces South African blacks, named 'Operation Uncle Remus'. A Machiavellian plot, it envisages a kind of Final Solution to the race problem. In the event of a revolt by the blacks, tactical atom bombs would be used with the secret connivance of the Americans, the English and the Germans. Muller, one of the heads of BOSS, the South African secret service, goes to Bonn to negotiate the matter.

What led you to imagine such a scenario? Did you have any precise information?

I scarcely needed precise information. I had paid a month's visit to South Africa four or five years ago, to meet my friend, Etienne Leroux, a writer and farmer. (Etienne Leroux is a very liberal Afrikaaner, noted especially for a remarkable novel, *Seven Days at the Silbersteins*.) I like to know the countries I bring into my novels, but 'Operation Uncle Remus' is the product of my imagination, and the idea seems to me quite logical. I wrote in the Introduction that if this type of secret planning did not exist at the moment, it would certainly come into existence before long. I don't believe the fine anti-apartheid words of the United Nations and the West. Whatever our leaders say, they could not stand by and watch South Africa slip into enemy hands. The country occupies a key strategic position on the Indian Ocean. If it became Communist like Mozambique, the Russians would be there, and no one in the Western camp can afford the risk of this happening.

A little after *The Human Factor* was published, the anti-apartheid movement brought out a book called *The Nuclear Axis*. When the South African embassy in Bonn moved house, these people had found crates of secret documents in a garage; the documents revealed the existence of an 'axis' established between West German and white South African military and scientific personnel. They had formed contacts in order to set up a nuclear alliance ... so I had been right to send Muller to Bonn.

Pure coincidence?

Yes, because I hadn't read *The Nuclear Axis*, which was published several months after *The Human Factor*. At any rate, one knows of the existence of American stations in South Africa for satellite guidance. The elements of an 'Operation Uncle Remus' already exist, not excluding the laws which allow anyone to be thrown into prison on the pretext of an inter-racial relationship when in fact the person has been arrested for knowing too much, or for engaging in espionage or resistance.

I must tell you I've had no contacts with dissidents, but one must not under-estimate the number and influence of liberal Afrikaaners. It must be indirectly thanks to them that *Travels with my Aunt* and *The Human Factor* appeared in South Africa: the publishers took the trouble to change the jacket for *Travels with my Aunt*, for they were aware that if the blurb had disclosed that Aunt Augusta had a black lover the book would fall foul of the censor. In fact it never did, any more than *The Human Factor*, which is rather stranger. Vorster already perhaps had enough literary problems with the contradictions in his own government: one of Leroux's books *Magersfontein, Oh Magersfontein* had been awarded an official prize and had immediately been banned. The publishers appealed and lost, but this didn't annul the prize already awarded. So the government had other things to worry about than to ban or censor my books.

The racial problem in South Africa was one of the important political questions raised in The Human Factor. *But it seems to me that what really haunts this book, beyond the theme of gratitude and love, this 'total risk', is the theme of the human being hypnotised by Moscow. Maurice Castle in this novel, like the priest hunted by God in* The Power and the Glory, *seems to be insidiously snared by the ideological machine.*

Why are you, Graham Greene, still so fascinated by Communism, and perhaps especially by the defections or the 'betrayals' in the West?

Or the East. It is not betrayal or defection that interest me, but what goes with it, a sort of waning faith. I am interested in the moment when a man reaches 'the dangerous edge' where faith wavers. I have a great friend, a Hungarian Communist. One day he came to see me in Paris, and I thought I detected this dangerous edge. He told me that he had read *The Quiet American* and had gone to the British Council in Budapest to find out about a poet, one 'Clogg', whom I quoted as an epigraph to *The Quiet American*.[1] No one knew anyone of the name of 'Clogg'. I explained to him that the poet was Clough, an agnostic of the Victorian era, whom I'd always liked, especially his poem, *Easter Day*, with the refrain after each verse, 'Christ is not risen.' I had the idea of showing him three lines that I'd underscored in pencil. I wanted to watch his reaction.

[1] I do not like being moved: for the will is excited; and action
Is a most dangerous thing; I tremble for something factitious,
Some malpractice of heart and illegitimate process;
We're so prone to these things, with our terrible notions of duty.
                                        A. H. CLOUGH, 1819–1861

They were:
    Of all the people under heaven's high cope
    They are most hopeless who had once most hope,
    The most beliefless who had most believed.
I had aimed truly. He betrayed no emotion, but I knew that
he understood my motive.

VI

Certainties

Having uncovered the 'devil's advocate' in Graham Greene, one could hope to come to closer grips with him and to predict his movements precisely by locating the place where the devil lurks. But the difficulty is only compounded, for he turns out to be unfaithful to the very devil, and to his own disloyalties. He refuses to play the advertised role for the good reason that he has no role to play. Contrary to what one might suppose, he will not, whether for the fun of it or on principle, be party to a game of hide-and-seek. Besides, he comes to a stop right in the middle of the road. One believes he is going to turn aside, but the 'floating wall' abandons its evasions to become an impregnable fortress. Then he will sometimes adopt positions which are apparently incompatible with the man of the Left which he rightly claims to be. The real paradoxes surface of their own accord, especially when he is discussing the Irish or Palestinian question—though he will speak with a certain caution and even abandon fixed positions in favour of a further evolution in his thinking. So it is not entirely true that he speaks up for the underdog: he might fairly be accused of succumbing, like Scobie in *The Heart of the Matter*, to a questionable pity which can degenerate into a sort of ill-considered favouritism.

His compassion, his sympathies cannot be universal or systematic. Why should he not, after all, be a man like any other, with his prejudices and even an occasional touch of latent xenophobia? He admits to never having been attracted by the Arab countries and describes how, during his first journey in Liberia, one of his really odious porters was a Mandingo, a Muslim, who aroused in him 'a few prejudices reinforced today by the fanaticism of that horrible old man Khomeini'.

What in fact is surprising is the sharpness of his commitments, however unexpected these may be: asked about his role during the Spanish Civil War, he says he was quite undecided at the outset, for Franco repelled him, but the attitude of the Republicans did not satisfy him either. (He had earlier explained that, here too, as a Catholic, he could not tolerate the atrocities committed against Spanish Catholics.) So, rather than abstain from the conflict, he wanted to help the Basques, for with them, at least, the choices were simple and unambiguous. After taking the train to Toulouse, from where a little bi-plane was supposed to fly him in to Bilbao, besieged by Franco's forces, he found himself at six in the morning at logger-heads with the pilot, who refused to take off as he had been nearly shot down on his last mission; so all Greene could do in the end was to return ruefully to England.

Graham Greene has therefore always been at one with his time. Today he says it is Latin America that interests him most. On this subject his position is scarcely paradox-ical. His profoundest hope is that the Somoza clan will not regain power with American support. His journey to Nicaragua in August 1980 (at the invitation of Tomas Borge, the Minister of the Interior) reveals an observer impressed by the success of the revolution and angered by the assassination of young Sandinistas sent into the mountains to teach the peasants to read.

The author thinks that his political viewpoint is scarcely

different from what it was in the 'thirties; he cannot see why it should have evolved, for he remains faithful to the precept of Tom Paine according to which 'we must guard even our enemies against injustice'. These two examples of his interest in what is afoot—in Spain and Nicaragua—selected at random, do suggest a further question: if writing and action have evidently been so inter-dependent, how is it that such a substantial schism between political commitment and literature is tolerated?

Politics do not serve literature any more than literature serves politics, Graham Greene explains. Many aspects of his life and work none the less (and this is not the least of the paradoxes) seem fated to deny this assertion. Graham Greene's novels, by their very directness, depend on reality, a sort of reality which in turn relies on fiction for its subsistence and perception.

Does one then have to accept this new element of mystery, just as one has to understand the writer amid his welter of complicities?

So you like to find in others the double allegiance of the dog who has two masters. Is it not the perpetual movement between doubt and the absence of doubt which seduces you, rather than faith itself?

Perhaps. Everything that moves interests me – whether it's an individual or a nation.

Change for the sake of change?

Not in the least. I like to be where a genuine change may take place, a fundamental upheaval as in Cuba or in Chile before the fall of Allende. I hoped for something to shift in Europe, with Dubček for example. England would interest me more if it were not stifled in its everlasting parish-pump mentality. As a result, I've only voted once in my life, for it was not easy to feel enthusiasm for any particular party. The Labour party under Wilson and Callaghan was a catastrophe, so was the Conservative party under Heath. The Liberals hardly existed. As for the Communists, they have no place in our parliamentary system. But I think that Mrs Thatcher at least has the virtue of honesty, which was not the case with Wilson and Callaghan. One might try giving her a chance.

Even so, did you not criticize her sharply in The Times *on 15 September 1980 about British arms sales to Pinochet's Chile?*

Yes, it was a rather personal attack. I nicknamed her 'Thatcher-Zaharoff', after the notorious arms dealer, Sir Basil Zaharoff, who had been active after the First World War. I also allude to him in one of my early books, *A Gun for Sale*: at the time, a Royal Commission was holding an enquiry into arms sales, which came to nothing, as might have been expected. Nowadays the State profits just as shamelessly from the international arms race, and moral sense has gone by the board.

I recently wrote deploring[1] a similar absence of scruples on the part of the Foreign Office in sending one of its representatives, Mr Ridley, to Guatemala (one of the most bloodthirsty military dictatorships in Latin America), to discuss the sovereignty of Belize over the heads of its citizens. Its Prime Minister, George Price, was, in the opinion of the Rightist opposition, a 'Communist' with leanings towards Cuba. I met Mr Price on a visit to Belize two years ago and I know few people less likely to join the Communist camp. Certainly Price is a Socialist, but equally he's a practising Catholic—and in his youth he

[1] Letter to *The Times*, 13 August 1980.

almost became a priest. I lend little weight to the rumours spread by the opposition in Belize: during my stay there they announced the arrival of a 'so-called writer called Green (*sic*), Communist agent of a foreign power'.

Once again, it is curious to notice that you take the side of the underdog. Could you not become a little less romantic with age? Who would get overheated today about Belize?

You don't realize the situation. Overheated? There you've said it—Belize is a powder-keg. It has fewer than 200,000 inhabitants, but it is about the only country in Central America where the Left has managed to retain power. From the strategic angle the stakes are high. Belize has welcomed a large number of political refugees from Guatemala; to discuss a 'compromise' with Guatemala would be to sign their death warrants. Moreover if Great Britain gives up a part of Belize's territory to its neighbour, who is to stop Mexico from pressing its own claims to another section? Then what will be left of Belize?

You have already taxed me with 'romanticism' in connexion with Panama. What you take for romanticism is in fact simply a state of alertness. Besides, I don't see why an interest in what moves should diminish with age—after all, I too am moving: I travel a great deal, I continue to make friends. I am drawn to others, I try to be ready to take sides even if occasionally my partisanship seems at first glance disproportionate to the event, or even contradictory.

I think it's through my books that the paradoxical nature of certain commitments are most clearly seen. But I don't feel I am in conflict with my work. When I consider my books in that light, I don't reject a single one of them. The contradictions spring from me, not from my books.

Is that not rather the same thing?

No: I don't express all my contradictions in my books— a few I keep to myself. I don't think that *The Quiet*

American leaves any trace of my private ambivalence as between my pro-French and my pro-Viet-Minh sympathies. Bear in mind, though, that when I say that I keep certain contradictions to myself, that is not altogether true. I must have expressed my doubts clearly enough to have had Marshal De Lattre accuse me, once at dinner, of being a spy, and to have had my every action scrutinized by a Sûreté man. (That was 'Monsieur Dupont', on whom I played some dirty tricks, poor man.)

There's nothing in my books, either, to hint at my feelings for Fidel Castro, about whom I'm very much in two minds: I admire his courage and his efficiency, but I question his authoritarianism.

Nor have I exploited the experience that I had in Chile in 1971, for history has tragically borne out my fears about Allende's ability to conquer the difficulties which awaited him. I was fond of Allende, I felt relaxed in his company and that of the Chilean leaders at the time, but I distrusted his political sense.

I've told you that I find it hard to be a hundred per cent behind someone or a hundred per cent against him: if there is one moral principle clearly in the forefront of my mind it's Tom Paine's assertion that 'we must guard even our enemies against injustice', whether it's perpetrated by a democratic government or by a dictatorship.

But you are not always on the side of the feeble or the desperate: why did your sympathies not extend, for example, to the Communist insurgents in Malaya?

I did feel some pity for the poor devils and their sufferings in the jungle, but I felt on the side of the Malays, who were for the most part against the Chinese Communists. The guerrilla leader, whose name I've forgotten—he must be very old if he's still alive—had been decorated by George VI after the Second World War. What the Chinese were attempting was to destroy the country's economic infrastructure, the rubber plantations and the communications system, especially the railways.

The guerrilla warfare began to peter out when the Chinese, who were not pro-Communist, withdrew into the villages and established centres of self-defence against the rebels who were terrorizing them (just as the provisional IRA is nowadays terrorizing the Catholics in Northern Ireland).

When I went to Malaya, the idea was to cut their supply-lines so as to make their life in the jungle increasingly difficult. At the same time, the government ran an effective propaganda campaign promising a peaceful, happy life to those who surrendered. The 'losers' were given a sort of safe-conduct to protect them from possible discrimination or vendettas.

My younger brother Hugh was in charge of psychological warfare, so I had all the easier access to the documents the Communists left behind them. Some of these were quite pathetic. The shadow of Mao Tse Tung loomed behind the manuals in which love was discussed: 'How to deal with love.' 'Is illicit love to be countenanced?' These questions were touching, they were so remote from reality; so were the exercise books left behind by a rebel who was so young he was still a school-boy.

The conditions in the jungle were unimaginable. I only spent three days in it, with the Gurkhas. The point is that in this country it never stops raining. There is no 'rainy season'—there's just rain. The smell of the jungle is ghastly. Everything's rotting. When one comes out one stinks to high heaven until one's had a bath and changed one's clothes. It was so unbearable, even for three days, that on the first night I came close to putting a bullet through my temple. The Gurkha detachment I was with was hunting two hundred guerrillas who had been scattered by an air strike. There were only thirteen men in the patrol. And I thought, 'If I haven't the stamina to endure this'—I was then over forty—'and they have to detach two men to take me back, I'll put a bullet through my skull. That will at least save them the bother.'

Was it really such hell?

Yes. One was sucked by leeches. One covered about one mile an hour, because while the English regiments followed the paths through the jungle the Gurkhas advanced in a straight line—they thought this would give them a better chance of coming upon the insurgents. One had to cross mountains over four thousand feet high; the mud clung to one's boots, and one had to hang on to the branches to avoid falling. In three days one had covered twelve miles without running into the Chinese.

That was my experience of the jungle. Later I spent a few days with a Gurkha tank regiment, then in a railway station in the state of Pahang, the nerve-centre of the guerrilla war. I completed my *reportage* by staying with a rubber planter.

Did you take part in any actual clashes?

No. Once, we came upon the body of a young Malay, which we loaded onto one of the armoured cars. He had been run through with a bayonet. He must have been cycling to the nearby factory, because when we got there all his workmates ran out and put a cushion under his head. The Chinese workers stood in the background, giggling. I indignantly asked the officer, 'How dare they behave like that?' He told me, 'It's nervous laughter; they're scared stiff.' How strange it all was.

Was Malaya one of your main preoccupations, in 1951?

Not particularly. *Life* had sent me there. I took advantage of this to escape from certain private worries.

What kind of worries?

I can't say. There are some things I can't talk about because they also concern other people.

1951 coincides with The End of the Affair ...

More or less. Perhaps we can get back to the real questions?

You have just alluded to the provisional IRA in unflatter-ing terms. In view of your habitual partialities, and bearing in mind the fact that you are a Catholic, should you not be on their side, on the side of the underdog?

But who is the underdog in Northern Ireland? I have great sympathy for the Catholics, especially because they are the real victims of the Provos. The Protestants can at least protect themselves and hit back. My lack of sympathy extends only to the terrorists in Ulster and to the Provos. The Provos are not the underdog. They are the executioners, just as Reginald Maudling was, with his 'deep interrogation'—he made me ashamed of being an Englishman.[1] At that moment I protested against the actions of the Conservative government in Northern Ireland.

To return to the IRA, I think that many people still have some picture of the old-style IRA which existed during and

---

[1] See the letter of 26 November 1971 to *The Times*, in which Graham Greene attacks Mr Maudling, the Home Secretary, and denounces the 'deep interrogation' used in Ulster jails: 'If I, as a Catholic, were living in Ulster today I confess I would have one savage and irrational ambition—to see Mr Maudling pressed against a wall for hours on end, with a hood over his head, hearing nothing but the noise of a wind machine, deprived of sleep when the noise temporarily ceases by the bland voice of a politician telling him that his brain will suffer no irreparable damage. ... How can any Englishman now protest against torture in Vietnam, in Greece, in Brazil, in the psychiatric wards of the U.S.S.R., without being told, "You have a double standard: one for others and another for your own country."'

after the First World War. I do admire that IRA, but the Provos have turned into out-and-out gangsters, devoid of ideals. One might as well be in Chicago. They bully little shopkeepers who, unless they give way, are punished by knee-capping. They terrorize the Catholics. They own the taxis. They own the big self-service stores. They win fortunes thanks to terrorism.

And yet the extreme poverty of the Catholics who provide their recruits is no secret, is it?

The Provos aren't poor. I can't stand the sentimental drivel they evoke. I realize that terrorism is practised on both sides. I'm just as averse to Protestant terrorism. In fact it's no longer a question of 'Protestants' versus 'Catholics' but of two terrorist gangs. The only man who can walk through Belfast in perfect safety, I'm convinced, is Paisley. The Provos will never attack him—he's their best ally.

So although I'm in sympathy with several of the freedom-fighter movements round the world, I think a distinction has to be made between 'armed combat' and 'terrorism'. Here's an example to illustrate the distinction. A Sandinista I met in Panama came to see me at Antibes. I asked him, jokingly, 'Haven't you made a mistake in taking the National Palace at Managua? Wouldn't you have done better to take a Pan Am airliner at the airport? That way, you would have held a whole group of Americans hostage and put pressure on Washington.' His answer was, 'No, that would have been a terrorist act.' The Sandinistas have always behaved very correctly. The real—the official—terrorism was carried out by Somoza.

And yet there are times when you seem to approve of a certain form of violence.

Violence is an inevitable consequence of the state of the world we live in. I think that the 'guilty'—I speak of them

(115)

in an essay called 'At Home'—is all of us. We belong, to quote the words of Ezra Pound, to a 'botched' civilization. But I don't approve of violence *per se*.

Five years ago, you disengaged yourself from the Palestinian question with a single sentence, 'As for the Palestinians, I think that Arafat's visit to the UN is an enormous farce. Logically all the members of the UN should have stood up and burst out laughing. I am pro-Israeli . . .' Have you changed?

Possibly. My feelings are considerably tempered now with Begin. I don't think it's I who have changed, it's they. In Dayan's day, there was reason to hope for an Arab–Israeli *rapprochement*. I can give you a small but significant personal instance. In 1967, Dayan invited me to dinner in Tel Aviv; we went to eat, not in a Jewish restaurant, but in a little Arab one.

For some while after the Six Day War I was totally in sympathy with Israel, for I believed that she was still gravely threatened in spite of her lightning victory. Today some of my sympathies are with the Palestinians, because I don't see what chance they have of real autonomy so long as Begin remains in power.

You have told me that when you write you have no reader in mind other than yourself. Is there not a contradiction here between certain political commitments and your work as a writer, which is accomplished rather egoistically?

A political commitment has never served as motivation for a book of mine. I don't believe that political action is part of a writer's function. In my view he is no more than an observer and I don't think I've gone outside the framework of my functions. I've seldom, anyway, been given the opportunity—except perhaps in the Cuban revolution, when I was able to make myself in a small way useful. I can't see any other instance.

Your memory sometimes seems to let you down most conveniently! Admit at least that you may have had a political influence on people by the slant of your books, if only in making them aware of the 'human factor'.

I've had a certain influence inside the Church, among priests, but I don't think I've ever had the slightest influence politically. As I don't belong to any party, I've no chance of putting this question to the test.

Can you not judge by the response of your readers?

Impossible. One does not know one's readers; one does not know what impact one makes on them.

Does that not bother you?

No, because basically I'm a writer, not a political thinker. I hold sentimentally to Tom Paine's dictum, for example, which remains valid in all circumstances. But I have no message to convey.

How do you react when you are regarded as an anarchist?

That depends on what you mean. One of my great friends, Herbert Read, was an anarchist. For him, anarchy meant reducing a system of government to its smallest possible entity, for instance, even villages should be self-governing. I don't think one can achieve a total elimination of centralization. In that sense I'm not an anarchist. I, like most of us, am against the abuse of power while recognizing the necessity for a minimum of power. One is always opposed to the abuses of a Franco or of a Lenin.

Supposing you are accused of being a dissident?

That doesn't worry me in the slightest, provided that I'm allowed to be one in relation to the Conservative party, and in relation to many other things besides!

Do you not feel terribly isolated?

I can't see any harm in being a little bit isolated. It's not an unpleasant sensation, and I far prefer it to running with the herd.

*Well then, this question may perhaps seem 'below the belt':
when you take sides, is it not basically just in order to meet your
needs as a writer?*

By no means. Far from it. Most of the time, in this
domain, there are no literary motives—I don't regard my
reportages as literature. When I made my journey through
Mexico in 1938 with the intention of denouncing the
religious persecutions, do you imagine I knew I was going
to write *The Power and the Glory*? No, I'd never consent to
appropriate other people's political sufferings for literary
ends.

*But in that speech you made at Hamburg in praise of
disloyalty, you did say, 'a writer is driven by his own vocation
to be a Protestant in a Catholic society, a Catholic in a
Protestant one, to see the virtues of the capitalist in a
Communist society, of the Communist in a capitalist state ...'*

A character in *The Comedians*, Dr Magiot, was Communist *and* sympathetic, wasn't he? Even in the corrupt world
of *Stamboul Train*, years ago, I made Czinner—was that
his name?—an idealist. I like to give atheists a heightened
interest (I'm thinking of the doctor in *A Burnt-Out Case*)
by surrounding them by believers.

*Exactly. I was going to ask you whether this was not a little
too systematic ... a writer's trick?*

No, it isn't systematic. I don't think it's necessary to
adopt this attitude for each book. I have certain stubborn
idiosyncrasies, though, worse than 'writers' tricks'.

VII

Of Cats and Bumble Bees

When Graham Greene speaks of his writer's craft he gives a
lesson in simplicity to any who might expect him to come
out with learned dissertations.

As in his conception of the faith, here too he is quite
coherent in his preference for concrete principles over
dangerous and all-embracing abstractions. ('Abstract
expression has helped dictatorships to seize power.') He
shows how writing relates not to a miracle but to a fable—
that of the bumble bees and the cats, which he is later on to
explain.

A fable comprises a visual element, a story and a moral.
For Graham Greene the visual element are his characters,
on whom he fixes his gaze so intently that his eyes ache.
The story takes shape out of a mass of habits—the Martini
mixed with suitable decorum chez Félix is perhaps as
important as any researches into the theory of form. As for
the moral, it inclines towards the usual Greene paradox—
the paths of creation, however well signposted, are subject
to the laws of the unconscious.

Writing therefore remains a mystery. One realizes,
however, that it is the highly perfected result of a constant
labour of simplification. If he now admits that he derives
more interest and entertainment from gossip than from the
lucubrations of intellectuals (at whom he cocks a little
snook in passing), he does nonetheless read at least a dozen

of their publications a month—theological tracts, new Anglo-American authors, Darwin, P. G. Wodehouse, Volkoff, General Sir John Hackett, etc. His literary tastes and the depth of his analyses were already evident in his *Collected Essays*, and so was his talent for discussing the gifts and defects of others without jealousy or bitterness—a rare virtue in an artist.

Here the human side of his writer's preoccupations shows through: the frequent tussles with the blank page, with the temptation to use a word for its own sake, and touchingly evident too, the insidious fight against death, that 'unforgiving wall'.

He had said one day, 'I suppose I am a good popular writer.' The source of his writing (but only the source) is the adventure novel; what raises him though, in spite of himself, to the level of the greatest writers is the consummate lucidity of his style, a style as evasive as he is. For in a world where condescension is fashionable, he at any rate has been able to stoop without sentimentality to the level of commonplace sorrows, those within anyone's reach: the nail parings on the unmade bed of brittle love, the blood on the over-polished shoes of Pyle, the evening's whisky in which the double agent drowns his loneliness, or again that unhappy spider slowly suffocating beneath the tooth-mug—all these tangible shreds of life's absurdity and misery remind us with almost sadistic force of our own secret agonies. Greene forces an entry obliquely, in order to reach for what is universal.

You 'never commit yourself a hundred per cent'. And yet your loyalties sometimes seem to defy coercion. You have admitted that you are an extremist. Are you also a perfectionist?

I'm not a perfectionist in politics or in love. I try to be a perfectionist when I write.

How do you mean?

I aim to be content with what I produce. It's an aim I never achieve, but I go over my work word by word, time and again, so as to be as little dissatisfied as possible. I write not to be read, but for my own relief. My only readership is me. Novelists who write for a public are, in my opinion, no good: they've discovered who their readers are and, in submitting to their judgement, they're dishing things up like short-order cooks. But a writer has to be his own judge, for his novels contain faults which he alone can discern. The harshest judgements should be his own.

I've only asked the opinion of friends on one or two occasions. I sent *The End of the Affair* to the writer Edward Sackville-West and he told me that he didn't much like it, but that I ought to have the courage to publish it, as the Victorian writers did, without worrying whether it would be deemed better or worse than my previous novels. So I followed his advice.

The second instance was to do with *The Human Factor*. I no longer knew what to think of it, because I'd set it aside unfinished for so many years that I felt uneasy about it. I wasn't sure if it mightn't be still-born. So I showed it to my old publisher, Frere, who had retired; he had been a friend of D. H. Lawrence and of many other notable figures of the past. I was sure he would give me an honest opinion. I explained to him that I should be perfectly content to put the book away in a drawer, leaving it to my children to get it published after my death if they wished.

He wrote back that he'd rather discuss it with me in person and, as he was going to be in the South of France anyway, he suggested stopping in to see me at Antibes. I took him out to lunch by the port. As we talked of this and that I thought: he's going to give it the thumbs down. In the end I hesitantly asked him, 'Well, what is your verdict?' He answered, 'Why, publish it of course—it's one of your best!' I was very surprised.

But as a rule I'm quite clear about what I've written: I know when it's good or bad. I know, for instance, that I find it difficult to render action. That's the hardest thing for a novelist. Hemingway managed it; (he wrote *The Sun Also Rises* fifty times). A street-fight is harder to put across than our conversation. So is the notion of time. Take *Stamboul Train*: it was not a great success from that point of view. I had to compress time for the sake of the action.

Your sympathy for the failings in other novelists is surprising, especially in your Essays. Should you not have a little more indulgence for your own?

The writer builds on the foundations of his own deficiencies: a deficiency is often a blessing. The honorary consul, despite his defects, succeeds in loving. He succeeds thanks to his failings. To return to action, I had an unfortunate tendency to encumber it with adjectives and adverbs, which slowed the pace. Nowadays I manage to convey the illusion of action—but I still don't describe it.

One can also be aware of a fault without being able to put a finger on it. It's quite infuriating. I remember the trouble I had tracking down the defect in a play, *The Potting Shed*, which in any case I'm not fond of. At the time, in 1956, it really bothered me. I was on another visit to Malaya (but not during the Emergency). And I only discovered the flaw after I'd smoked a pipe or two of opium. Thanks to the peace and quiet these afforded me, I was able to mend the play. Let me assure you, though, this isn't my normal method of work. It's just an amusing example.

You cannot write and escape from yourself at the same time, can you?

For me at any rate, opium did not really represent a way of escape. I fell in love with opium the first time I had a whiff of it on a staircase in Haiphong. The high French official who was my host took me later to a *fumerie*. After that I smoked it regularly but in small doses. I found it helped when I had to travel without sufficient sleep, for instance, when I had to take a military 'plane between Hanoi and Saigon at dawn. Before these rather special journeys I'd forgo dinner and alcohol and visit a *fumerie*. After a few pipes followed by a few hours' sleep I felt as refreshed as if I'd had a full night's sleep.

Have you taken dope before, to write?

Yes, in 1939. I realized that war was imminent and that soon I'd have to leave my wife and children. We'd hardly put aside a penny, so I had to finish a novel in a hurry to bring in some income while at the same time working on *The Power and the Glory*. I devoted my afternoons to this book which was coming along very slowly. In the mornings, I got to grips with a thriller, *The Confidential Agent*, which was completed in six weeks under the influence of benzedrine; (in those days it would take me at least nine months to finish a book). Breaking the habit was not easy; I only succeeded by progressively reducing the dosage. I couldn't break the habit straight off, for the craving set my nerves on edge. I've been wary of benzedrine ever since. There is a less drastic stimulant, dexadrine, which I also used occasionally. But now I no longer take anything.

How do you 'work'?

If one wants to write, one simply has to organize one's life in a mass of little habits.

Like the dry Martini before meals?

Yes. This goes back to the days after the war, when I worked as a publisher, till 1948. I had to have lunch with authors, and the idea of listening to these dreary people talking about their books right through a meal persuaded me that I had to give myself a boost to endure this drudgery.

Later I abandoned the dry Martini. I've gone back to it again, but with variations: in the summer I tend to take a gin and tonic in preference to a whisky. Or else I revert to whisky.

It cannot always be easy to maintain one's little habits when one is travelling!

In Panama, it was rum punch ... one manages to survive, you see, if one's the least bit adaptable.

Where writing is concerned, I'm even more obsessive as it's a question of life and death. Writing has to develop its own routine. When I'm seriously at work on a book, I set to work the first thing in the morning, about seven or eight o'clock, before my bath or shave, before I've looked at my post or done anything else. If one had to wait for what people call 'inspiration', one would never write a word.

Is it true, while we are on the subject, that you count your words?

Yes, always. It's a pity I don't have a manuscript with me to show you.

Do you have a device for counting?

No, I count them all up with my finger. When I'm hard at work, I try to keep to a minimum daily word-count.

Is it not quite abstract, this counting of words?

Not at all. A chapter contains so many words, and one wants to know exactly how one chapter balances another by its weight in words.

For me it's also a way of forcing myself to work; I used to set myself a quota of at least five hundred words a day—which doesn't mean that I never wrote more. My quota has dropped to three hundred; when I reach this number I note it in the margin. You'll find my manuscripts peppered with little crosses and the annotation 'six hundred', 'nine hundred', 'twelve hundred', etc. I know by and large how long a book will be when I finish it. With *The Human Factor*, for example, I calculated that it would weigh in at 110,000 words, more or less—and it came out at 110,300. Laugh if you will—but that's how it is. I feel as though there's a kind of calculator inside my head. Words are important: books are made out of them.

But there are long words and short words!

I know that in France you tend to calculate on the basis of letters. That simply wouldn't work in my system. My imagination wouldn't accept it.

As for my 'productivity', I used to write a book in nine months, as I said, but now it's one every three years. I'm writing more slowly and I'm spending more and more time on holiday.

A few moments ago you spoke about how your imagination and your unconscious functioned in relation to words. In some of the Introductions to the Collected Edition of your works you mention your chance encounters with your own characters, whom you seem quite surprised to run into. And yet the style and structure of your books give the impression that you are a writer in total control. How do you reconcile the foreseen and the unforeseen, the unconscious and the conscious?

The 'craftsmanlike' aspect of my work is a very conscious one. I pay attention to the 'point of view', for instance, and I re-read aloud what I have written, making a good number of corrections for the sake of euphony.

On the other hand I've mentioned the character of Minty in *England Made Me*. He was quite a minor character to begin with, but he suddenly asserted himself almost to the point of taking charge. In all my novels I'm content to have blank spaces which I don't know in advance how to fill. The characters are thus able to follow their bent more freely. That's why the novel is, to my mind, more interesting than the short story: the novelist reserves for himself surprises, which he can't afford to do in a very short story which is conceived almost entire before the writing has begun.

When I started to write *Travels with my Aunt*, I didn't expect to be able to finish it. (This is rather unusual, because generally I can at least anticipate a beginning, a middle and an end.) I'd embarked on this adventure for my own amusement, with no notion of what might happen the next day. A number of ideas I expected to use in short stories became recollections of old Augusta. I was surprised that they all cohered into a logical sequence, and that the novel became a finished product, for I'd been regarding it more as an exercise based on the free association of ideas, though I had it clearly in mind that it was to be 'a book written for the fun of it . . . the subject is old age and death'.

So one shouldn't speak too much of technique or craftsmanship. I place great reliance on what I take to be the unconscious, no doubt because of my experience of psycho-analysis as an adolescent.

This isn't to say that writing is magic; magic does take a hand, though, in little touches—the right element to make the various parts cohere drops into place at the proper time without my realizing it. One has to be borne up by a sort of faith in one's unconscious; one has to maintain good relations with it. One enters into contact with this side of oneself by means of dreams and of those unexpected elements which slip into a novel, and one becomes aware of the role played by the unconscious only at the instant when it materializes, surreptitiously.

So you have to feel yourself almost innocent before your writing?

No, I never feel myself innocent, not even when I'm amusing myself. What d'you mean by 'feel oneself innocent'?

To have the sensation of discovering certain things, to be caught unawares...

Oh yes, indeed, this happens with every book. For example Castle, the double agent in *The Human Factor*, finds at one point that he needs to talk to someone. He goes into a Catholic church. In the confessional there's a priest who treats him abysmally and suggests that he go and see a psychiatrist. Castle comes out of the confessional, and at that precise moment he realizes that he has come face to face with a man as lonely as he is.

I had not anticipated this scene, and I liked it. The priest was not after all gratuitously disagreeable. This took me completely by surprise, because I'd started out with the idea of satirizing a certain kind of priest.

Do you not yourself cultivate this sense of the unreal which these unexpected developments bring about? One has the feeling that your stories are sometimes tales for adults written for your own benefit. I am thinking especially of that strange story in which a sick man returns to the home of his childhood and sees, as he is about to go to sleep, the adventures of the little boy who had gone for a walk 'under the garden'. What is the meaning of this dream inside a dream about a dream? Is it just a story which you took pleasure in writing?

Oh, I never 'take pleasure in writing'. But I did perhaps free myself temporarily from the tensions of reality, or rather from too realistic a way of writing. No doubt I wanted to go back to my childhood, because the house depicted in *Under the Garden* is similar to the one in which we spent our summer holidays. There was also a pond with an island in the middle—and when I went back many years later, like the narrator in the story, I discovered that there was no need for a raft or a boat to take one across to the island. A jump was all that was needed, for the pond was scarcely bigger than a puddle. The gardener, on the other hand, was still the real gardener. I make the same sort of escape in a passage in *The Human Factor* in which Castle, the adoptive father, tells his son the story of the dragon which hides on the Common and only comes out in order to visit him in school.

Another childhood memory?

I never knew a dragon, but as a small boy, I knew of plenty of caves which might have been its lair, because the Common was riddled with trenches dating back to the First World War. Incidentally I nearly broke my neck on several occasions when I went riding on this furrowed Common of Berkhamsted.

These flights into the fantastic, into what you call 'fantasy', to which you return, notably in Doctor Fischer of Geneva, *what do they represent for you?*

I don't really know. Perhaps you're right: I'm escaping. For example, if one can remember an entire dream, the result is a sense of entertainment sufficiently marked to give one the illusion of being catapulted into a different world. One finds oneself remote from one's conscious pre-occupations.

What in your work is the proportion of 'entertainment' to these 'conscious preoccupations'?

I really couldn't say. In my earlier books I didn't permit myself many of these flights. The sense of entertainment crops up for the first time in *Stamboul Train*, and more markedly in *England Made Me*, but it doesn't come fully into the open until after 1945. I've noticed, in working on the Introductions to the Collected Edition, that all my humorous stories date from the Second World War, as though the proximity of death provoked this irresistible urge to laugh and to 'unwind'. *Travels with my Aunt* was also written when I was well up in my sixties, in the awareness that I was gradually approaching the wall that does not give way.

In Under the Garden *you say that there are two important things in life, 'laughter and fear'.*

It's not I who say so—it's the narrator, Wilditch. At that time, 1962–3, I probably shared his view, for I was Wilditch as I wrote. Today—I don't know. I'm no longer in the same situation that he was in. He was afraid of dying of cancer, and I'd come out of hospital where I suffered a bronchioscopy, after contracting a bad attack of pneumonia, because the doctors thought I might have lung cancer.

When you take note of an aphorism, bear in mind that it expresses the views of the character, which may for the time being coincide with those of the author, but which may be meaningless twenty years later. Nowadays I think that laughter is the important thing, or at least a smile—nothing is worse than a giggle. In fact, I shouldn't speak of laughter so much as of the importance of a certain sense of fun. For example, a play I've just written, *For Whom the Bell Chimes*, has no object but to make people laugh. It's a sort of farce.

Why this sudden need to amuse?

It was an idea I'd jotted down some time ago. I keep a file of ideas and dig into it, usually in order to write a short story. As I had no novel in mind at the moment, I looked into my file and found a sketch I had quite forgotten. I wrote this play very quickly. A play is much easier to write than a novel, possibly because I'm not basically a play-wright and so I'm less self-critical.

The theatre gives you entertainment—but has it influenced you as a novelist?

I think it's a necessary release from the solitude of being a novelist. The advantage with a stage play is that I only work at it for six weeks, which is little compared with the two or three years devoted to a book. There follows the work of 'carpentry' which I really enjoy: one removes or adds a bit here and there to meet the criticisms of the director and actors. One attends the rehearsals. There one has to take care that the actors don't distort the rhythm of the play. The theatre is a release. I had recourse to it early on—I started at sixteen.

But I don't see that the theatre's had any direct influence on my novels. I've always enjoyed writing dialogue. I think I'm quite good at it.

What are the writer's 'conscious preoccupations' you mentioned earlier on?

I don't obey any particular rules. There are, of course, basic principles to be observed: adjectives are to be avoided unless they are strictly necessary; adverbs too, which is even more important. When I open a book and find that so and so has 'answered sharply' or 'spoken tenderly', I shut it again: it's the dialogue itself which should express the sharpness or the tenderness without any need to use adverbs to underline them.

Your style has grown much simpler, has it not, since A Burnt-Out Case?

Even earlier. It gradually became simpler with *The Quiet American* and *The End of the Affair*. My first books were very bad, full of metaphors which I chose for their extravagance, influenced as I was by my readings in the 'twenties, when I was very attached to the English Metaphysical poets of the seventeenth century, who devoted themselves to highly complex rhetorical exercises.

Today my early novels horrify me, they're so absurd. There's nothing worse than poetic prose.

Do you live with your writer's tics or do you resist them?

I don't know my tics. Which ones d'you mean?

Well, your insistence on never describing your characters directly. One never 'sees' the face of Querry, or Castle, even though you give other information about them.

I wouldn't call that a tic. When I read a novel and have to commit all those details to memory—she's a red-head, she has a long nose, she wears her hair in this way or that, and so on—I get annoyed. I prefer leaving the reader to do this work, to form his own image, so he doesn't have to worry about forgetting if a character's hair is straight or curly.

Among the rules to observe, you have mentioned the 'point of view'. How do you conceive it?

I think that during a scene one must always place oneself in the 'point of view' of a single character; this doesn't totally exclude the author, whose viewpoint may emerge in a metaphor, a comparison or what-have-you. But if you have a scene involving several characters, and you describe it first through one person's eyes, then through another's and so on, the whole structure of the scene becomes muddled and loses in intensity. This happens now and then with writers whom I'd call 'secondary'—and invariably with bad writers.

Henry James managed to maintain the same point of view throughout an entire book, at the risk of seeming artificial. Proust cheated. He chose to present his books in the first person, but his 'I' described scenes and conversations which he could not have witnessed. It's a great failing in Proust—on a grand Proustian scale—for the narrative occasionally lacks credibility. Only God and the author are omniscient, not the one who says 'I'.

Do you have a feeling of spying on your characters?

Yes, very much so. When I construct a scene, I don't describe the hundredth part of what I see: I see the characters scratching their noses, walking about, tilting back in their chairs—even after I've finished writing—so much so that after a while I feel a weariness which does not derive all that much from my effort of imagination, but is more like a visual fatigue: my eyes are tired from watching my characters.

It is strange, for in your novels one visualizes the action very well without there being properly speaking any visual elements.

True, there aren't many. Not enough. It's a criticism I should make of my books. I don't know why I have this failing. Perhaps it's because, as I write, I'm projecting these scenes in my head. So I can't see any need for writing 'she sat down' because I know that that's just what she's done. I think the readers can make their own descriptions. Let them. I prefer to read Dickens without the Phiz or Cruickshank illustrations, marvellous though they are.

You were film critic for The Spectator *from 1935 to 1940, and also for* Night and Day[1]. *What impact has the cinema had on your books?*

When I describe a scene, I capture it with the moving eye of the cine-camera rather than with the photographer's eye—which leaves it frozen. In this precise domain I think the cinema has influenced me.

Authors like Walter Scott or the Victorians were influenced by paintings and constructed their backgrounds as though they were static and came from the hands of a

---

[1] As a result of an article in which Greene remarked that Shirley Temple's seductiveness was of a more adult nature, the actress, then aged six, brought a suit for libel against the magazine, which met a comic, though unfortunate, end.

Constable. I work with a camera, following my characters and their movements. So the landscape moves. When I turn my head and look at the harbour, my head moves, the houses move, the boats move, don't they?

I realize the extent of this influence of the cinema, especially since *It's a Battlefield*, which contains many descriptions which were supposed to be cinematic. This goes back to long before the period you're alluding to, because films and film reviewing interested me very early. I started writing film reviews for a paper I edited at Oxford in 1924, the *Oxford Outlook*, in the era of the silent screen. But the impact of the cinema on my way of writing comes from the films themselves rather than from my reviewing. In those days I was a very keen cinema-goer, but now I've practically lost interest, I don't know why. Perhaps it's because one has a better grasp of an art form which coincides with a given period of one's life. Thus I don't often read the poets of two or three generations after mine. I think, too, that we grow less adaptable. We become fossilized ...

So would you be, in this sense, a man 'of the 'thirties' as John Le Carré said?

No, because I've made films in the 'forties, 'fifties and 'sixties. But the time comes when one's enthusiasm begins to slacken. One's left with only enough enthusiasm for one's own work, which is writing novels.

In your books, do you see in colour, or in black and white?

It's hard to say—as with dreams. I realize that I've dreamt in colour when I remember the colours, so I assume the other dreams must have been in black and white—but who knows?

Take G. K. Chesterton: he describes nature very flamboyantly. In his pages a sunset is practically like a chromo. Incidentally, he wanted to be a painter—that's something I lack. I think I see the world in black and white, with an occasional touch of colour.

That is like your way of seeing human nature, which you describe in The Lost Childhood *as 'not black and white' but 'black and grey'. Would there be some correspondence between your ideas and your sensory perception of the world?*

I'm ready to believe so.

I expect I am quite wrong, but you do not give the impression, apart from the cinema, of interesting yourself in the plastic arts or in painting.

Oh but I do—I love painting very much indeed. I go to exhibitions, I buy pictures. I have a special interest in painting.

In your Paris apartment you have a number of Haitian primitives.

Yes, they're amusing folk paintings. But I also have pictures by a man I profoundly admire, Jack Yeats, the poet's brother. I have works by Henry Moore—a water colour, and a bronze statuette, the Warrior, of which I am very fond. I have a work by Graham Sutherland, and here at Antibes I have paintings by two Cuban artists, a Hungarian, a Pole and a Panamanian!

Forgive a sly question: have you always liked paintings, or have you acquired the taste along with fame—and money?

As far back as I can remember, I've always liked paintings.

But you do not really like objects.

What do you mean by 'objects'?

As I look around in your apartment, I see very little bric-à-brac, statuettes, little souvenirs.

Little souvenirs . . . Look: this carved stone here on my table comes from Yugoslavia. They say the stone is five million years old. Weigh it in your hand.

But you do not have many, not even on your table.

There's a whole mass of little oddments up there on a shelf!

Are my remarks annoying you?

Not in the least. I have two shelves crammed with little oddments—look at them!

Even so, you are not really fond of objects—

—What sort of objects are *you* attached to?

Me?

Yes, what sort of 'little oddments' are you attached to?

Oh, wood sculptures, lots of objects . . .

Personally I don't much care for wood sculptures.

. . . and Indian bronzes.

Well, I have Henry Moore's bronze warrior! That's a little object—very little. There are lots of little oddments here.

Even so, I was surprised when I entered your apartment in Antibes.

Why?

I was expecting a different framework, something less cheerful because of the legend which attaches to you. One expects to find greyness everywhere, fog, dingy armchairs. Now these armchairs seem to be new!

Well, fairly new. I bought them about three years ago. They're certainly newer than my suits—I've been wearing them for twenty years.

Do you feel that you have perfectly mastered your technique, or are there still some grey areas?

I'm not aware of any.

You were saying, for instance, that you had some difficulty in conveying action.

Yes. To begin with. Not now though, probably because I side-step the difficulty by reducing action scenes to the minimum.

Your characters, do they not sometimes refuse to come to life?

That's not a problem. There are always one or two characters who rebel, but that's almost necessary in a sense; if they all lived with equal intensity, the novels might become over-crowded. One needs a background on which to project silhouettes who don't necessarily have to take a leading role. I think I get over the technical difficulties well enough.

In that case, why were you so unsure about The Human Factor?

I don't think that it's one of my best novels. It's merely adequate. But perhaps I've under-estimated its qualities. For a writer, the bad elements stand out like a boil. It's all very well to recognize that a boil is only a part of the body, it's still disproportionately obtrusive. My favourite book, the one that bothers me the least, is *The Honorary Consul*, and no doubt the next is *The Power and the Glory*.

Why The Honorary Consul?

Because I've succeeded in showing how the characters change, evolve. *The Power and the Glory* was more like a seventeenth-century play in which the actors symbolize a virtue or a vice, pride, pity, etc. The priest and the lieutenant remained themselves to the end; the priest, for all his recollection of periods in his life when he was different, never changed. The action was contained within a short time-span.

Now in *The Honorary Consul* the doctor evolves, the consul evolves, the priest too, up to a point. By the end of the novel, they have become different men. That's not easy to bring off, but I think that in this book I've succeeded. But I found writing it hard work; until one reaches a certain point one has to work very hard and with complete lucidity. Then something happens which is rather like an aeroplane taking off; one drives on and on down the runway, suddenly the 'plane leaves the ground, picks up speed, rises into the air—at that moment one feels a sense of victory. One may have to stay at the controls, but the worst is over.

I knew well enough how I would tackle the last chapter of *The Honorary Consul*. I had all the material I needed. Plenty of choice. It wasn't organized by my mind, but it was all there, and I relied on my ability to set it down on paper. And yet the wretched book seemed never to take off. It kept rolling along the runway even when the last chapter was approaching. Only when I'd actually finished the novel and discovered that the end worked as I wanted, only then did I realize that we had in fact, quite unwittingly, taken wing a long time before.

Do you think it is preferable to maintain a certain degree of unconsciousness in order to write a novel?

Yes. I can't stand being made too aware when people highlight obvious links between my novels. After all even Shakespeare repeats himself. These repetitions are necessary and unavoidable, but they need to remain buried in the unconscious of the writer.

My first novels, *The Name of Action* and *Rumour at Nightfall*, were bad because the romantic young author I was at the time was too recognizable in the characters. A writer has to conform to two conflicting requirements; he must be involved in his novel and detached from himself. One detaches oneself in the course of merging into the characters. One doesn't think, 'Would I do this or that?' One notes that 'Smith has done it'. One doesn't even say, 'How would Smith react in this or that situation?' because Smith acts on his own account. One simply forgets one's own existence.

It's not so much a question of taking leave of oneself, if

you like: it's more a case of taking leave of one's conscious 'I'. Telling one's dreams to a psycho-analyst every day gives one the same sensation: while the dreams are a part of oneself, in reciting them one has the illusion of their being part of quite another life. Books and dreams have that much in common, I suppose.

What is your relationship with your characters?

I try to be as detached from them as possible. When I feel that the book is on the point of taking off, that the story is coming to a life of its own, I can feel that the characters have a will of their own.

I would be a poor father to them, at all events, for I tend to leave them to their own devices. I've told you that I don't re-read my books, except when they're going into a new edition and I have to check them for misprints. Otherwise they are locked in a cupboard in my room. I don't even keep them on a shelf. I also have an entire cemetery of abandoned books, or rather, of fragments. I used to throw them out. I can see perhaps two or three worth exploiting at a pinch—but I'm a little doubtful. One of them would be based on my experiences in Panama. The second is called *Getting to Know the Captain*. The story opens in Berkhamsted, but as I've already used my childhood background in *A Sort of Life* and *The Human Factor*, I think it would be cheating to use it again. Writing a book which one has held in reserve only becomes necessary when it's getting in the way: *The Human Factor*, for instance, with its twenty thousand words, kept coming back like an albatross to hang round my neck while I was writing *The Honorary Consul*. So I had to get rid of it before moving on to other novels.

What do you do with your first drafts? Do you revise a great deal?

I correct my first draft until even I can hardly decipher it. Then I record it on dictabelts and send it to my secretary who types it out. Afterwards I correct the typewritten copy over and over again until I have to record it on dictabelts again. Sometimes I repeat this operation at least four times. Between the manuscripts and the final typed version I achieve a half-dozen drafts all corrected and recorrected to the point of illegibility.

So a book is put together little by little, in a painstaking fashion while the unconscious is simultaneously at work. That's why I get down to work first thing in the morning and only come back to it in the evening, after an aperitif and a half-bottle of wine. Then I set about corrections, relying on sleep to enable me to complete the work in the morning. I re-read my morning's work just before bedtime, to stimulate my unconscious—or my subconscious if you prefer—in the hope that it will sort out the problems. In practice the unconscious, faced with secondary difficulties (stylistic or structural in any given chapter), accomplishes its task like a good parent, one who has first inspired the book and now sees it through to the finish.

I choose the title, usually, right at the beginning, before I start writing. This means that I have a precise idea of what the book will turn out to be—except for *Travels with my Aunt*, as I've said, and the thriller *The Confidential Agent*, written under the influence of benzedrine.

If your unconscious seems to be a reliable companion, you yourself sometimes give the impression of cheating him: you introduce him into your novels and then pretend not to recognize him. You take pleasure in dropping your characters into symbolic moulds: Charlie Stowe, in I Spy, *goes down into his father's shop and hides under the counter; Wilditch explores below the earth in* Under the Garden; *The Third Man takes us into the sewers of Vienna ...*

That's something I've never noticed. Can you give me other examples? You've given me only three!

You say you have never noticed! And yet is not I Spy *a sort of caricature of Freudian symbolism?*

It was an example rather than a caricature. I certainly had Freudian elements in mind. As for the Vienna sewers, there's nothing exemplary or symbolic about them: they were quite prosaically the sewers of Vienna.

At least admit that you are aware of the incredible sense of anguish which is found in your novels. How do you explain it?

I'm not conscious of it. I don't go out of my way to communicate it to the reader. How do you expect one to be able to notice a trait which is so much a part of daily life? I can capture anguish when certain characters betray it, at certain points in a novel, but I don't recognize it as a constant in my books. This is not to say that you're wrong, but once again, I don't want to be confronted with the pattern in the carpet: it would become too much of an obsession, I think.

Anguish is a contagious disease. Does it not bother you if you infect your readers with it?

Well, I suppose it is perhaps contagious . . .

In that case, the result seems to be a little negative.

Oh, I wouldn't say that a contagious disease is something negative. Where a virus develops in your blood it's very positive—very active. If I found myself in battle and poison gas was being used, I wouldn't consider the gas as a negative element. Surely it's a very positive weapon.

How do you mean?

Because the gas will kill me. It's most effective. I'm sorry to tease you a little when you say that an illness is negative. Health, now—there's a negative thing: one is in a state of flat calm, one has nothing to fight. The negative can be pleasant, the positive can be unpleasant. I found that boredom was a neurosis until it provoked me to positive

(140)

action. But one doesn't react immediately. The negative phase can last a long time ... whole days when there's nothing but boredom.

You see why I might be glad to contaminate my readers with anguish? One is more likely to discover love in the midst of war, courage where there is danger.

But why this fascination with horror and the obnoxious?
What do you mean?

You once gave up reading Joseph Conrad, did you not, in order to free yourself from this fascination for 'the heart of darkness'?

That was not the reason. I simply realized that Conrad was having a disastrous influence on my style. I caught myself plagiarizing the worst devices of his worst book, *The Arrow of Gold*, where his own style had been influenced by Henry James's.

In your Essays, though, you seem to be equally attracted by James and his way of anatomizing the mechanisms of human behaviour in all its horror.

That's true. Most people will tell you that James liked to describe delicate scenes of picnics on English-style lawns. One of my reasons for liking Henry James is his sense of corruption and horror.

I couldn't go back to Conrad until I went to that leper colony in the Congo. I took with me *The Heart of Darkness*, for I told myself: 'Now I have my own style, my own way of seeing things. I'm safe from this influence. I'm cured.'

Have you been much influenced by your contemporaries?

No. Never an intellectual influence, just one of friend-ship, like Evelyn Waugh's, and he attacked me now and then. But his opinion counted for little—less than my own.

In the domain of writing you seem in fact to follow the

'labyrinthine ways'[1] *you have traced out for yourself, in an obstinate solitude. This leads us straight into another paradox: you say you have 'betrayed a great many things' in the course of your life (I think you are alluding to your sentimental life)* ...

Yes, I'm sure I've been a bad husband and a fickle lover!

That is what I was going to ask you: how can you admit that and yet show such stability as a writer?

I suppose one can work very hard to accomplish a certain task—writing—and that as a result one can't be a very diligent husband or lover.

Perhaps writers are fickle by temperament, because the individual who finishes a novel bears little resemblance to the one who began it. One lives so long with one's characters that they tend to influence one. For instance, my last bout of depression, my worst, I think, coincided with the gestation of *A Burnt-Out Case*. I can find reasons for this in my private life, but also in my two-year cohabitation with the deeply depressive Querry, with whom I never in fact identified myself.

The fact is, one is changed by one's own books. The writer plays God until his creatures escape from him and, in their turn, they mould him.

So you think you are very different from the man who wrote The Power and the Glory?

Oh definitely. I'm much older. Life changes us a little more each day, doesn't it? I'm not the man I was two years ago. One's eroded. Time nibbles at us bit by bit, stone after stone.

But do you recognize yourself in your books?

No: I never revert to them, never give them a thought, unless I'm compelled to, as now.

[1] *The Labyrinthine Ways* was the provisional American title of *The Power and the Glory*.

The critics, too, ought to be a little more inclined to forget what one has written previously, but they always expect one to remain absolutely constant. I suppose it's easier for them to decree that I'm a 'one-book man' than to recognize that change happens. This is why *Travels with my Aunt* was poorly received in England, while I consider it one of my best books. I expect similar reasons lie behind the general refusal to grasp the importance of fantasy in my books. No one's ever questioned me about it or really commented on it. When *A Sense of Reality* came out, the title, which was meant to be ironical, was taken at face value. It seemed to me rather amusing to apply the word 'reality' to a book which was so remote from it. I served up quite a new dish—but nobody noticed.

The intrusion of dreams and fantasy into my other books has been overlooked in the same way. Few critics remarked on the dragon scene in *The Human Factor*, or the fable told to the young woman by Querry.

There are several types of 'fantasy' in your books.

Yes. Some, like *Travels with my Aunt*, are escapist while others try to cure anguish by giving it a symbolic representation: *Under the Garden* evoked fragments of my childhood (that's always a wrench) and the painful recollection of a recent operation. So I don't exactly escape by writing them down; on the contrary, I tamed certain nightmares in making use of them as a background. Even though it's a less personal book, *Doctor Fischer of Geneva* is more or less in this vein.

It is strange that you, who say that you want to escape from yourself in your writing, should have endowed these fantasies or these stories with very recognizable elements of your private life. But perhaps these creations correspond to periods when you were in fact at peace with yourself . . .

I can't remember ever having been at peace with myself, except for brief spells.

In one of your Essays you write: 'Most men have one earth into which they can creep to rest the nerves'. Do you, also, have an 'earth' in which to hide yourself and find peace?

I wasn't referring to myself. I don't know whether I hid in an 'earth' . . .

Then what do you do?

I crouch in a corner like a sick dog. I don't want other people's sympathy. I go to the doctor, but I don't want any 'ministering angels' around me.

You wrote The Living Room *in 1953. Why did you come to the theatre so late? Was your interest deflected at that point from the cinema?*

No, I don't think so. I was a theatre critic during the war, but I went back to writing screenplays. However, the theatre was my 'thing' when I was sixteen. I went back to it in the early 'fifties because the subject of *The Living Room* had been haunting me for too long: I was obsessed with this house, whose rooms were condemned one by one as an occupant died. So I suddenly said to myself: 'Here's a new drink that I must sample, even though I've been eyeing the bottle for years without touching it.' So I poured myself out a glass, and I drank the theatre to the dregs.

You had just written The Third Man *and* The Fallen Idol *(1950). You were embarking on your novel about Indo-China. With the theatre, did the 'fifties represent your most fruitful period?*

My most creative period, I suppose you might say, was the 'thirties, when I published the most books—when I could bring out a novel in nine months, with the next one already substantially formed in my mind. After the war it took me much longer to bring out a novel. But I don't know how one is to measure creativity—it's the result, I mean the quality, that matters. By this standard I think my books were better after the war. I was better pleased with what I wrote—but then I was also more dissatisfied with myself, more critical of my work.

Are you pleased with your plays?

I'm pleased with *The Complaisant Lover* and *The Return of A. J. Raffles*. I don't like *The Potting Shed*. I've a weakness for *Carving a Statue*, which was mauled by the press. Actually I don't regard myself as a playwright; I'm no more than an amateur—six plays in twenty years is not enough.

I do think, though, that my books have inherited one thing from my plays: dialogue is becoming increasingly important. In a novel, I prefer it when description takes second place to dialogue. To compare a mole-hill to a mountain, Henry James wrote two novels, all in dialogue, in a period when he was writing essentially for the theatre. His plays enjoyed no success, but his work luckily is stamped with the theatre.

Your plays seem to me to be only the skeletons of your books.

That's because on stage you cannot afford to squander words. You have to simplify. Besides, you haven't seen them played—perhaps you would think differently if the skeleton had been fleshed out by actors.

It's this very metamorphosis that fascinates me: an actor, without changing a word, can ruin a play or bring it to life. I've seen an accomplished actress playing the wife of Rose's lover in *The Living Room* against the advice of the director and sending the audience into giggles because she insisted on playing for sympathy when she ought to have been faithful to her initial role of shrew. I have also seen an actor come on stage so drunk that he made up his lines, and

I was the only one to notice. In *The Return of A. J. Raffles* the actor playing the Prince of Wales looked so much like Edward that I had the impression he had come out of his tomb.

The theatre lends itself to whole-hearted tomfoolery, to pranks and ribaldry. One quickly achieves a state of euphoria. That's why I've started another play which will be quite mad: I don't believe I've time enough to start a new novel.

What makes you think so?

I hope I don't have much time left. I shouldn't want to live to ninety.

You told me that the Greenes are very long-lived.

Yes, I know: that's the danger.

You will always be associated with The Third Man. *The cinema, even more than the theatre, has marked your work. You did once recognize that you are 'no doubt a good popular writer'. Are you to literature what crime films, Westerns, the Marx Brothers (whom you like) are to the cinema?*

My books don't in fact make good films, and when I write a novel I never think about whether it might adapt to the screen. The only book written with the screen in mind, *It's a Battlefield*, was never made into a film. The only good films, *The Third Man* and *The Fallen Idol*, are those which I wrote as screenplays. The rest were nearly all made in America and were, with one exception, deplorable. As for *Our Man in Havana* and *Brighton Rock*, this may sound pretentious, but all that saved them was the fact that I took a close hand in their production. One might have expected Fritz Lang to make something interesting out of *The Ministry of Fear*, but he was reaching the end of his career, he was short of funds and made do with a ready-made screenplay—for which he apologized to me.

To return to your question, though, my books can't be 'popular' in the sense applied to so-called popular films, otherwise they would have been easier to screen.

In what sense can they, then, be considered popular novels?

They don't sell as well as the works of Mr Forsyth or Mr Hailey ... But I'm sure I've had better luck than many writers who could be considered good.

When readers say that they are transported to 'Greeneland', everybody understands that they are referring to a kind of atmosphere which you have succeeded in creating. When a paper uses the headline 'Our Man in Antibes', the allusion to Our Man in Havana, *etc., is grasped at once. What do you think of that?*

I've acquired a certain popularity which many another author deserved. This is partly because I'm a storyteller, unlike writers of the previous generation such as Virginia Woolf and E. M. Forster—who complained, in a study of the novel, 'Oh, a story, I suppose we have to have a story ...' Well, I've always enjoyed telling stories, and my impression is that readers prefer this to the *nouveau roman*, for instance. The life-expectation of the *nouveau roman* has turned out to be limited. I like Robbe-Grillet very much, but I think that certain experiments in writing can't be extended beyond a rather limited number of years.

But luck does play a large part in an author's popularity.

Do you not believe that your success is due to an absence of sophistication?

I try to write more and more simply, but I don't believe that this makes for attraction, quite the contrary. The really popular books are full of clichés, people 'flushing with anger' or 'going pale with fear'. Popular authors bring nothing new to their readers, and I have no wish to belong to that type of popular writer.

On the other hand, I wouldn't want to belong to an

intellectual élite. I don't dislike intellectuals. I have friends who could be called intellectual. But to my mind the intellectual is often academic and sometimes a shade pretentious.

Does culture form a part of this pretentiousness?

Like Goering, when I hear the word 'culture' I reach for my revolver.

And yet you are a cultivated man!

I've read many books, I've written many books, but that's not what you call culture. I hate the word. It clothes another of those abstractions I find repulsive.

Have you suppressed the distinction between your 'entertainments' and your novels in order to escape an excessive popularity?

No. I established the distinction originally in order to escape 'melodrama'. (I've subsequently concluded that melodrama isn't all that baneful.) Anyway I told myself—wrongly as it happens—that if I occasionally wrote what in England is termed a thriller, in the manner of John Buchan's *The Thirty-nine Steps*, which I greatly admired, the ensuing novel might be free of melodrama.

I started making this distinction with *A Gun for Sale*. I'd even considered writing under another name, but my publisher warned me, 'We can't give you more than a £50 advance, because in that case you're a new writer on the market.' So I gave up the idea and classed the novel as an 'entertainment'. The last one to be conceived in this category was *The Ministry of Fear*: after that, novels and entertainments resembled each other more and more. *Brighton Rock*, for instance, started in my mind as a thriller. From the first sentence, my intention was to write a crime novel, but the novel eventually moved in quite a different direction. But the most absurd case, I think, is *The Quiet American*. I recently came across the manuscript, which one of my publishers kept in his safe. The first page is entitled, 'Novel Number Thirteen—Entertainment'. I really can't understand how I could ever have seen this book as a simple thriller.

I abandoned the dichotomy once and for all with *Travels with my Aunt*, for it served no further purpose.

Could you stop writing?
No.
What keeps you going?
The need to accomplish a worthwhile task, a 'desire in search of a desire', perhaps? A neurosis brought on by habit rather than by despair. An irresistible urge to pinch the abscess which grows periodically in order to squeeze out all the pus.

Are you not afraid that these childhood sources may eventually dry up?
Do you mean 'writer's block'? At the beginning of the 'block' one says to oneself, 'This time it's the *coup de grâce*; it's the end.' A few years ago, the Hungarian writer Tibor Dery confessed to me that he'd recently fallen victim to writer's block. I asked him, 'For how long?' 'Ten days,' he told me. (He was 82 then.) My own block had been going on for months! At the door, when I saw him out, I suggested that he pray for me—he was a convinced Communist and never prayed. His reply was that it was enough to drink three glasses of whisky, sit down in front of a sheet of paper and start writing. I've never tried: I think that in my case it would take a good deal more than three glasses.

Only dreams enable me to fight these painful blocks. One dreams four or five times a night. I've trained myself to remember my dreams. In periods when I can't write I keep a notepad beside my bed. When I wake up in the night

(149)

I note the dream down at once. I've discovered that dreams are like serials—the instalments sometimes carry on for weeks. At the end they form a whole. I've included some dreams, like *The Root of All Evil*, in short-story collections, and others in novels.

I work closely with my unconscious, but I still don't understand how it functions—what is the origin of my writing, the manner in which it comes to me—even though I know more or less what's going to happen. I have magical places in which to work—Capri, for example, these last thirty years. There I can do more in three weeks than I could in three months at Antibes. I also used to like working at Brighton, no doubt because of the crowd of memories which surrounded me there.

How do you discover your characters?

I don't know. *The Honorary Consul* originated in a dream which had no connexion with the book, but the little seed germinated and gave my novel its first impulse.

Are you inspired by people you meet?

No: I think that the main characters always have to exist somewhere within the writer. I might conceivably draw secondary characters from acquaintances, but they're never the motive force of a book.

But your question about characters reminds me of a page from Darwin's *Origin of Species* which I was re-reading a little while ago. I had been reading it first when I was writing *Under the Garden*, with a witch-like character called Maria; beside the words 'wild plant' I'd scribbled the name 'Maria'. She is a Darwin-borne character. Further on I'd underlined a whole passage where Darwin explains that bumble bees abound near towns and villages where there are cats. The reason is that the cats eat field mice—and field mice are enemies of bumble bees. Around these villages, certain plants grow more abundantly than in places where there are no cats. This is because where there are no cats, the field mice decimate the bumble bees, who used to fecundate the plants. The presence of the plant is indirectly related to the presence of cats.

The same is true of characters and creativity. It seems as difficult to trace them back to their origins as it is to trace back the link between the plant and the cat.

VIII

The Poor Little Night
in the Big Trees

So many articles and even books have been written on the
way in which Graham Greene understands Catholicism
that to begin with he was not even prepared to talk about it
here.

Is he Pelagian, Jansenist, Augustinian or what? It has
been said that he followed Hilaire Belloc and G. K.
Chesterton in rekindling religious controversy in Great
Britain. He evidently disapproves of being so classified,
and honours such as these make him smile. He merely
concedes that his books may perhaps have helped sharpen
the focus on certain principles which govern belief.

Catholicism for him is a private affair—not to be
discussed. Nevertheless he reflects the image of a tormen-
ted, wavering but ineradicable faith, the product of his
paradoxical universe. It appears all of a sudden like a poor
little night in the big trees. The big trees of corruption, evil
and failure threaten the transparency, peace and fragility of
the night. But, with battles at an end, it is the night which
prevails, the poor little night which steals in among the big
trees until he gives expression to a terrible fundamental
doubt: 'I'll have it sorted out soon enough,' he says, 'or else
I won't.'

In his preface to the French edition of The Power and the Glory, *François Mauriac says that you have 'stolen as it were like a thief . . . into the Kingdom of Grace'. You are very discreet about your conversion in* A Sort of Life; *what you do say about it seems by its very 'banality' to contradict Mauriac's remark. Did you become a Catholic the way one falls in love?*

No, I needed convincing arguments for the possibility that God exists. I'm very fond of an Anglican divine, Bishop Gore; he was also a writer, and he opened one of his books with the words, 'The hardest thing is to admit the existence of God.' I'm with him there. I was perfectly ready to accept the historical existence of Christ, but how was I to start from a hypothesis as vague as that of the omnipresence of God?

So you were an atheist?

No, but religion bored me to death with its Sunday services and its endless readings from the Bible.

Anglicanism meant absolutely nothing to me, no more than Buddhism or Catholicism. One of my grandfathers was a clergyman with a great sense of personal guilt, so one day he had defrocked himself in a field and ended his days in an asylum. You see, I've inherited some bad genes. I too rebelled, but not from a sense of guilt. At Oxford one had the choice between having breakfast sent to one's rooms if one attended the morning service in chapel, or of going to breakfast in the hall. I opted for the second solution.

Your rebellion did not go very far!

That's because I was so indifferent. I knew nothing about Catholicism; it was a closed book to me. It was a long time later, when I was working in Nottingham, that I slipped a note into a collection box in the cathedral, asking for instruction because my fiancée was Catholic. I wanted to understand what she believed in, I wanted a better grasp of the nature of her faith. I had no thought of becoming a convert myself.

So would love have been responsible for your conversion?

I've told you, my conversion was not in the least an emotional affair. It was purely intellectual. It was the arguments of Fr Trollope at Nottingham which persuaded me that God's existence was a probability.

How do you explain this success?

I enjoyed our discussions. I was stubborn as a mule, but he got me interested in his game. Subsequently I plunged into books of theology, which fascinated me. You see, I wasn't in the position of a Protestant who is searching for an alternative. I believed in nothing. Fr Trollope and I saw each other regularly for six months, sometimes at the cathedral, sometimes on the open upper deck of a bus, when we'd pursue our arguments for the entire journey. (When I was baptised, I made it clear that I had chosen the name of Thomas to identify myself not with St Thomas Aquinas but with St Thomas Didymus, the doubter.) I eventually came to accept the existence of God not as an absolute truth but as a provisional one.

So you could not say, like Sarah in The End of the Affair: *'I've caught belief like a disease. I've fallen into belief like I fell in love'?*

I should have been pleased if my faith had been like hers. But I must say in my defence that unlike her I had also to be converted to the idea of Christianity.

When did you begin to 'feel' your faith?

I recognized the first inroads during my visit to Mexico in 1938. It's all bound up with my loyalty to the underdog—and so it has been ever since. In Mexico the underdogs were the Catholics. When I heard a woman tell of the death of one of her family, how they had to send in secret to the capital for a priest to come and celebrate the funeral rites in Tabasco (the persecutions did not affect the inhabitants of Mexico City, who were in a way 'protected' by the tourists); when I had witnessed the fervour of the peasants, who would go back and forth on their knees across the flagstones of those churches in Chiapas which were still open (though not to priests), and who would kneel for ages with their arms outstretched as though crucified—I tried to pray this way, and I found I could keep my arms up for a few minutes, perhaps, no longer, while they would stay as though crucified for the entire service; when one has been with believers who suffered for their faith—the masses said in secret in Chiapas, and Tabasco, where there were no longer either churches or priests—this endowed the Church with such grandeur, the fidelity of the believers assumed such proportions that I couldn't help being profoundly moved. I expect I'm explaining myself badly. I would compare these worshippers with the polite little congregation in Chelsea, which I sometimes joined, and the ladies in hats, and I'd feel that religion was the peasant approaching the altar on his knees, his arms outstretched as though crucified.

Did you not have a feeling, at that time, of betraying your family, your Church, your compatriots—by contempt?

Not in the least: before my conversion I had no Church. My family was quite indifferent to these problems. As for my fellow-countrymen, so long as I was unknown, they never knew that I had become a Catholic. When *Brighton Rock* was published, the critics thought that I was profiting a little from my position as a convert in order to tackle subjects out of bounds to others.

But did you not in 1938 have a sense of being torn between a form of superstition (as witness the Mexican peasant) and a belief of intellectual origin?

No. The two aspects coincided. I still believe in magic, even in the art of writing. If Catholicism has succeeded in reaching the remotest corners of Africa, it's no doubt because of certain magical characteristics. Its sense of magic is closer to the African than the abstractions of the Methodists and Anglicans. I'm inclined to find superstition or magic more 'rational' than such abstract religious ideas as the Holy Trinity. I like the so-called 'primitive' manifestations of the Faith.

What are they?

Oh, the ones I've been telling you about, and others which are harder to describe. One comes across people, for instance, endowed with a strange aura. I'm thinking of a friend of mind, a Spanish priest with whom I go travelling every year. He has a faculty for bringing people to life. He is not a conventionally pious man, but he is possessed by an absolute faith. When I asked him to describe it, he modestly replied, 'I do not believe in God, I touch Him.'

What do you think of miracles?

I want to believe in them. I have myself experienced what could be called a small miracle. I was in despair about someone—someone I had left rather brutally but whom I still kept seeing. The break was far from clean, and when we met we always ended up having an angry scene. So I went into a church and prayed to Padre Pio, the Italian Franciscan, to change the woman's attitude. From that moment all was calm. For me it was more striking than the sudden healing of a skin-disease. Perhaps it was coincidence, but I like to think that it was magic.

I have also seen with my own eyes the stigmata on Padre Pio's hands, in the South of Italy. He was not a man who looked as though he suffered from a nervous disorder. I was so convinced of his powers of goodness that I refused to approach him and speak with him. I explained to the friends who had brought me along that I was too afraid that it might upset my entire life.

As you see, 'superstition' made a late appearance in me. As a child and an adolescent I didn't know the meaning of the word. I only became superstitious when I started to accept the existence of God, and therefore of miracles.

And yet I have the impression, reading The Lawless Roads, *where you briefly mention your life at boarding school, that you would have had no need to become a convert, because faith was already manifested in you 'stripped of dogma', 'associated with violence, cruelty and evil'.*

Yes, I was ready to believe in the existence of evil. Many people are ready enough to accept the idea of heaven while they fail to notice the garbage at their door. Personally, though I have never believed in hell, the evil which surrounded me prepared me for the paradoxes of Christianity.

So is it through evil that one comes to religion?

You're asking a difficult question. What is 'religion' and what is 'evil'? I don't have an answer. Evil—others might call it misfortune.

A character like Pinkie in Brighton Rock: *do you not hold him up as the very incarnation of evil?*

I tried, as a sort of intellectual exercise, to present the reader with a creature whom he could accept as worthy of hell. But in the end, you remember, I introduced the possibility that he might have been saved 'between the stirrup and the ground'. I wanted to instil in the reader's mind a fundamental doubt of hell.

I wrote this book, however, before Hitler, before the concentration camps. My viewpoint might be different now, for even if one persists in rejecting the idea of eternal damnation, how can one deny the existence of total evil?

(157)

One has the impression, listening to you, that you are suffering more painfully than some the burden of a fate which appears to be investing us with its dark forces. Do you feel you are being crushed by what Cardinal Newman, whom you often quote, calls 'this terrible original calamity'?

Perhaps, with Hitler, and today the growing nuclear threat gives me almost the same sense of impotence before human 'malevolence'.

Is not your view equally darkened by the Christian consciousness of sin?

Not in the least. I don't like the term 'sin': it's redolent of a child's catechism. The term has always stuck in my throat, because of the Catholic distinction between 'mortal' and 'venial' sin. The latter is often so trivial as not even to deserve the name of sin. As for mortal sin, I find the idea difficult to accept because it must by definition be committed in defiance of God. I doubt whether a man making love to a woman ever does so with the intention of defying God. I always remember the example of a Dominican priest who found his life in Europe too easy and left for Africa, where he lived for years in a hut made out of old tin cans, only to discover that he was suffering from the sin of pride. He came back to England and confided to a friend that, during all this time of hearing the confessions of the faithful, he had never come across a single 'mortal' sin. In other words, for him, mortal sin didn't exist. The word 'mortal' presupposes a fear of hell, which I find meaningless. This being the case, I fear that I'm a Protestant in the bosom of the Church.

Then why do you say of Mauriac's characters that they 'sin against God'?

Because Mauriac's view of Catholicism was more orthodox. He did believe in mortal sin, so much so that the heroes of his novels really can defy God. I don't think that

(158)

Pinkie was guilty of mortal sin because his actions were not committed in defiance of God, but arose out of the conditions to which he had been born.

Do you think that writing has helped to strengthen your faith?

No, I shouldn't say so. My books only reflect faith or lack of faith, with every possible *nuance* in between. I don't see why people insist on labelling me a Catholic writer. I'm simply a Catholic who happens to write.

And yet you have created characters like the whisky priest, dogged by Grace; Sarah, called by God in The End of the Affair; *Scobie turning, in his pride and solitude, to Christ.* Brighton Rock, *with Pinkie and Rose (who is in a sense immaculate), symbolizes the battle between the forces of good and evil. These novels all treat the problem of the limits of divine goodness and of free will, the problem of corruption, too, in concrete terms. They display unexpected or unexplored facets of the problem: the sickness of pity, which one might call 'Scobie's complex'; greatness in decay, in the fornicating priest who is so possessed by compassion ... And the Church has recognized herself in your novels, even to the extent of condemning* The Power and the Glory *because you had broken certain rules in introducing 'paradoxical and extra-ordinary situations'. So Catholicism provides you with points of reference, though even these rules might be there only to be broken, would you not say?*

I've never willingly used these points of reference. There does exist a pattern in my carpet constituted by Catholicism, but one has to stand back in order to make it out. A great deal of time has elapsed between the various novels you've mentioned. Before *Brighton Rock* I wrote a whole series of books quite unconnected with religion. Lately I've drawn away from the subject again even though theology does make a fresh appearance in *The Honorary Consul* in the person of the guerrilla priest. I'm thinking also of *The Quiet American* in which suddenly, at the end, the journalist Fowler is sorry for Pyle's death and expresses a wish to turn towards something or someone to discharge his sense of guilt. In most of my novels one can find a religious influence.

But I refute the term 'Catholic writer'. Cardinal Newman, whose books influenced me a great deal after my conversion, denied the existence of a 'Catholic' literature. He recognized only the possibility of a religious dimension superior to the literary dimension, and he wrote that books ought to deal first of all with what he called, in the vocabulary of the day, 'the tragic destiny of man in his fallen state'. I agree with him. It is the 'human factor' that interests me, not apologetics.

I think, actually, that the whole argument in *The Power and the Glory* was deeply rooted in me from childhood precisely on account of the human factor. I remember members of my family coming back from their holidays in Spain, sometimes, terribly shocked because in some little village they had come across a priest living with his housekeeper, or keeping a mistress, and so on. I found their indignation exaggerated because, even though I wasn't a believer, I saw no reason why a man should not be different from his function, that he could be an excellent priest while remaining a sinner. I learnt to analyze the paradox of Grace more subtly after my conversion, from reading St Thomas Aquinas, St François de Sales, Fr d'Arcy and Fr Martindale (both English theologians)—but the paradox was an integral part of my universe.

Is that why you concede to people condemned by human justice the possibility of being saved 'between the stirrup and the ground'?

Yes: God's justice is not like that of a judge. It is a mathematical justice. (One talks of a just line.) It is very different from human justice with the distortions which witnesses, legal considerations, etc. can give to an ordinary judgement. God's justice derives from total knowledge. This is the reason why I don't believe in hell: if God exists—I'm not convinced He does—He is omniscient; if He is omniscient, I can't bring myself to imagine that a creature conceived by Him can be so evil as to merit eternal punishment. His grace must intervene at some point.

Would you allow a chance to such individuals as Papa Doc, Hitler and their like?

I'd favour the death penalty in their case, but the death penalty—even an eternal death penalty—is not hell.

In your novels you are content to substitute yourself for God!

All writers, even the worst, are led into assuming a role vaguely comparable to God's, for they create characters over whom they exercise almost total control. I should add, though, that a writer is even more like a double agent than he is like God: he condemns and sustains his characters by turns. Their relationship is so ambiguous that when the characters come to elude his control—as with Scobie in *The Heart of the Matter*—one doesn't know whom to blame.

You are a believer even though you say that you are only 'keeping a foot in the door'. In your opinion, does faith give an additional dimension to writing?

Human beings are more important to believers than they are to atheists. If one tells oneself that man is no more than a superior animal, that each individual has before him a maximum of eighty years of life, then man is indeed of little importance. I think that the flatness of E. M. Forster's characters, and Virginia Woolf's or Sartre's, for example, compared with the astonishing vitality of Bloom in Joyce's *Ulysses*, or of Balzac's Père Goriot, or of David Copperfield, derives from the absence of the religious dimension in the former. Mauriac's characters are equally endowed with this strange substantiality. In *La Pharisienne*, when one of them—a very minor character—crosses a school yard, we have a sense of having seen him in flesh and blood, while Mrs Dalloway doing her shopping leaves one indifferent. She moves out of our minds as easily as she moves out of Harrod's.

Along the same lines I should say that very few good writers have emerged from the Communist world, with the exception of a Solzhenitsyn or a Pasternak or a Sinyavsky, who have in fact retained their sense of the religious. The Welfare State has driven God off the stage, just like the devil, but it has failed so lamentably that I have the impression God is making a timid reappearance. History tends to prove that Faith is reborn from its own embers. Would a Solzhenitsyn have existed if Communism had met with a more obvious success?

That is the meaning of the question to which you have not replied: 'Is it through evil that one comes to religion?'

When evil achieves such a degree of perfection as to wear supernatural trappings, then it can rekindle faith in the supernatural. But extreme goodness has the same power. I've experienced it in contact with extraordinary men who were endowed with it—Padre Pio, whom I've mentioned, and similarly a priest in Indo-China; the Japanese had tortured him—they had ripped off his nails. He lived in a little hut not far from Dien Bien Phu. I don't know what's become of him. He said mass with anyone who passed that way. I have no model of sanctity in mind but I believe that man was a saint.

In your epigraph to The Heart of the Matter *you quote*

Charles Péguy: 'The sinner stands at the very heart of Christianity ... No one is as competent in the matter of Christianity as the sinner. No one, except the saint.' And concerning the paradoxes of Christianity you write in an Essay: 'The Christian inhabits a territory bordering on Good and Evil, and its bandit country.' Does Catholicism coincide so perfectly with human nature, as you see it?

That's what I used to think thirty-two years ago. I've not thought about it since.

Well, this vision of a world caught between two fires, a vision which is different from the dichotomy pervading The Man Within—*I was wondering whether it arose out of the influence of Catholicism.*

The Man Within was a beginner's novel, but I was already a Catholic. All my books, except for that dreadful collection of verse published at Oxford, were written after my conversion. My way of grappling with human nature has little to do with Catholicism; it derives from my experience of life, from what I can observe. It would be no different if I were a Buddhist. For me, the sinner and the saint can meet; there is no discontinuity, no rupture. I believe in reversibility.

But the basic element I admire in Christianity is its sense of moral failure. That is its very foundation. For once you're conscious of personal failure, then perhaps in future you become a little less fallible. I know a poem by Thomas Hardy which illustrates this particular consciousness of failure. May I read you part of it?

'You taught not that which you set about,'
    Said my own voice, talking to me,
'That the greatest of things is Charity ...'
    And the sticks burnt low and the fire went out
    And my voice ceased talking to me.

Your own voice seems to give you little peace.

That's true; especially at night. That's when failure stares me in the face. I've written some bad books, but I've also failed in charity, in compassion, and I've been cruel.

Is this the tribute which a 'spy of God', as you call yourself in one of your Essays, is bound to pay?

Did I say that? I don't believe it!

G. K. Chesterton, whom you so admire, and who is also a convert to Catholicism, did introduce into his books a God who plays the part of spy, or rather, of detective.

Not a God, Father Brown. They're not his best novels!

Are you still hounded by God?

I hope so! I hope so! I'm not very conscious of His presence, but I hope that He is still dogging my footsteps. I also find myself thinking, not so much that He is pursuing me, but that certain extraordinary circumstances have had a beneficial effect on my life—I don't mean in terms of professional success or in terms of money, but in terms of happiness. My life has been radically transformed by events which happened for no logical reason.

I perceive, then, certain conducting threads in this labyrinth; I assume they're not put there on purpose, but they are wound off under the eye of some sovereign power watching man's free will functioning. This power has simultaneous knowledge of past and future. The same phenomenon is given man in John Dunne's *An Experiment with Time*, in which he claims that during sleep dreams draw their substance from the future as well as the past, that the sleeper is in a position overlooking both. The omniscient God does not obstruct the functioning of free will, but He knows the past and the future—He has set their wheels in motion.

What is God like?

A mystery, an inexplicable force. That's why, when one

prays one shouldn't, in my opinion, address oneself to this inexplicable and mysterious force but to His intermediary, Christ. I think there's an element of truth in the myth about man being created in His image. But it is easier to pray to Christ than to an abstract entity. Human love can be only a pale reflection of the emotion that God must feel for what He has created.

As He appears in your novels, God is not as good as you are suggesting. Your literature is not that simple. It expresses conflicts between contradictory elements, between the hunter and his prey, loyalty and disloyalty. And yet nobody would dream of saying that you present a dichotomized universe, for these elements always have an obscure and disturbing way of merging. You, however, seem temperamentally poised on the dizzy edge of darkness rather than of light. Are you not fundamentally a Manichean who has never succumbed to his vice?

A Manichean believes that the world is wholly in the hands of God ... I mean of the devil.

Your first slip—do you confuse God and the devil?

Well, listen: in *The Honorary Consul* I did suggest this idea, through the guerrilla priest, that God and the devil were actually one and the same person—God had a day-time and a night-time face, but that He evolved, as Christ tended to prove, towards His day-time face—absolute goodness—thanks to each positive act of men. I thought I had invented a new theology for my dissident priest, so I was a little disappointed when my friend Fr Duran told me that this was all perfectly compatible with Catholic doctrine.

So you shuffle the cards in order to counteract an over-simplification.

On the contrary: I try to find simple explanations for complex phenomena.

(165)

Do you think that the Catholic Church today has at last 'rediscovered the technique of revolution', the absence of which you deplore in 1939 in The Lawless Roads, *which you wrote after your journey to Mexico?*

What lay behind that remark were the abuses of the Catholic Church in Mexico which had had the unfortunate result of bringing down on her priests the persecutions of the 'thirties. But the Church could no doubt be grateful for these persecutions: she was purged by them and is now in good health there.

I know that all too often throughout history the Church has sided with the powerful, but this has happened less frequently in the twentieth century. I think that at the moment, especially so far as Latin America is concerned, she has effectively rediscovered a technique of revolution. In Nicaragua, for example, the bishops aligned themselves clearly with the Sandinistas and two priests are in the government, while in El Salvador the bishops have united against the government and provided a martyred archbishop. The influence of Dom Helder Camara in Brazil is not to be under-estimated—though I know less of what's going on there.

In Europe it's still too early to pronounce on the surprising appearance of a non-Italian Pope whom I for one heartily admire. John XXIII was one of the most remarkable Popes we've ever had. Paul VI was a good and honourable man, but, strangely enough, he damaged the Church. He was too much influenced by the Curia, not sufficiently independent.

The present Pope inspires confidence because of his experience of life: he has worked in the mines, he has fought in the Resistance; he has a genuine political experience. I believe, moreover, that he is playing an important role in Europe's political geography—witness the warmth of his welcome in Ireland. The concrete effects are evidently not yet perceptible, but it's very possible that in the long run his visit there will have a valuable impact: he addressed himself to thousands of young people—very enthusiastic young people—and this may cut the grass from under the feet of the Provos.

His visit to the United States, on the other hand, was disturbing. I think it a pity that he raised the tired old question of contraception. In 1966, during the final session of the Papal Commission on birth control, nine cardinals and bishops pronounced themselves in favour of contraception—this proved that it couldn't be an intrinsic evil—and only three voted on the opposite side. It seems to me that one has to choose between that and abortion. I'm sure that most people are instinctively repelled by the idea of abortion, but abortion is very often nothing but the result of an absence of contraception.

What do you think of his rigorous stand on priestly celibacy?

There I'm in complete sympathy with him—though I know that it's not very well viewed at the moment. I think there has been too much laxity in this area. (Not that I'm the one to talk: when I became a Catholic I was very worried in case I turned out to have a vocation for the priesthood. I'd have made a very bad priest, for chastity would have been beyond my powers!) But if priests were allowed to marry, why not let them divorce as well? In that case, why shouldn't they marry four or five times, like Americans?

I think that for many people, especially the young, the priesthood must have the attraction of a crack unit. It's an organization which has to train for combat, one which demands self-sacrifice. I've nothing in particular against priests marrying—as you know, in the Eastern Catholic

(167)

Church marriage is permitted, a single marriage—but I'm convinced that the drop in vocations has to do with the fact that we don't put across clearly enough the attraction to be found in a difficult and dangerous calling. One enlists in a venture which is total. People are attracted to the Church where there's danger. I don't think there's a crisis of vocations in Latin America or in Poland.

You express yourself like someone seeing these problems from the inside.

Not altogether. Once again, I'm speaking not as a theologian, only as a writer who happens to be a Catholic, and perhaps even a Protestant inside the Church. For I've always considered it better to be a Protestant inside rather than outside.

Would you agree that you prefer your customary role of double agent to the pursuit of 'the Lord's work'?

What d'you expect? I was virtually born this way.

Then would you publicly defend Hans Küng and Edward Schillebeeckx, the 'heretics' of the Catholic Church today?

I would defend them as Christian theologians but not as Catholic theologians. I'm not in opposition to Rome. I know that in my books I've introduced characters— especially priests—who verged on heresy. (That's why *The Power and the Glory* was once condemned by the Holy Office.) But I've too often seen the absurdity, exemplified in the Anglican Church, of a bishop remaining a bishop even though he doesn't believe in the Resurrection, nor even in the historical existence of Christ. There are certain points of reference which cannot be abandoned, otherwise one might as well go and become a Buddhist or a Hindu. I believe in the necessity of a minimum of dogmas, and I certainly believe in heresy, for it's heresy that creates dogmas. In this sense heresy has great value.

So have Küng and Schillebeeckx!

Yes. They bring a new breath. I much admire Hans Küng, especially for his book *On Being a Christian*. Schillebeeckx is a great and very learned, very estimable theologian; but, as a barely practising Catholic, I find it very disagreeable when a historical event like the Crucifixion is turned into some woolly sort of symbol. The twentieth chapter of St John's gospel can stand with the best of eyewitness reports, and I don't see why Fr Schillebeeckx has to turn it into a symbolic sequence. If one considers oneself a Catholic, there is a certain number of facts which have to be accepted.

On the other hand if I were told that for some reason or other they had got it wrong about the Virgin Mary, or that the Trinity was no longer an article of faith, that would barely disturb my faith. The Trinity, for example, is nothing to me but a mathematical symbol for a mystery. One can talk about 'the communion of saints'—though I'm not all that sure of what it means. I believe in the existence of the saints. But the existence of the Trinity is to me of no importance: it illustrates an attempt to explain the inexplicable.

So would you agree with 'the new heretics' on a certain number of points?

I'm in favour of having these subjects aired, so long as one is not posing as a Catholic theologian but only as a Christian theologian. So long as differences between the Churches exist, those differences ought to be upheld, otherwise one becomes as foggy as the Anglicans. Catholicism has to remain human. A man lived: Christ. He lived in history. Why turn him into a concept, fit only for a handful of visionaries?

This debate shows that the Church is still on the move, that we're a long way from the Inquisition. Hans Küng is free to teach. No one has been excommunicated, not even, at the other extreme, Msgr Lefebvre. I think that, all in all, this controversy has enabled me to discover an amusing paradox, almost a Chestertonian one: while Fr Schillebeeckx's declarations were intended to make the unbelievable credible, they have had the opposite effect on me—they have suddenly revived in me a deep faith in the inexplicable, in the mystery of Christ's resurrection. And I don't think I'm alone in having reacted this way. Don't you think there's something like a small miracle of grace there for we who are semi-lapsed?

Your name has often been associated with Mauriac's. Do you feel closer to French Catholic writers than to your English colleagues?

I was very close to Evelyn Waugh, whose Catholicism was so orthodox that it clashed with mine. But, strangely enough, we never quarrelled in spite of substantial disagreements in the field of politics as well. Evelyn was conservative right down the line. I made him very unhappy with *A Burnt-Out Case*: he concluded from it that I'd lapsed from the Faith. We exchanged a sequence of letters on this subject, and our correspondence ended on a humorous note. Our friendship was deep, genuine, and in no way affected by the disparity of our ideas.

Among my contemporaries I appreciate Anthony Burgess. We have seldom met, but I admire his talent. I don't consider him a Catholic writer, though, any more than I consider myself one. The French press often couples our names because we are both labelled 'exiles'. (I don't have the slightest sense of living in exile.) The worst of it is that our names are also linked with Lawrence Durrell's, with whom I haven't the slightest affinity. The French are not always sound judges of English literature. Look at the way they took to Charles Morgan, who was held in small regard by British critics. (He probably read better in translation!) For me—perhaps I shouldn't say this—Lawrence Durrell and his cloying prose is the Charles Morgan of his generation.

To return to your question, I can think of hardly any Catholic writers with whom I feel an affinity. Bernanos, with his *Diary of a Country Priest* and *Diary of My Times* made a strong impression on me, but I discovered him after the war, too late to have been influenced by him. The same is true of Mauriac: the first book of his I read, *The Knot of Vipers* (this was before the war), didn't prove to be a determining encounter, though I was left the richer for it.

Did you know Jacques Maritain?

Not well. But it was he who saw to the publication in France of my first book, *The Man Within*, which he had slightly censored—or rather I received a letter from him asking me to modify certain 'sexual' scenes which he found too crude. I was very proud that even the French could be shocked by my prose, and so I gladly agreed to excise a few inoffensive little passages from the translation. But I never had any real ties with Maritain. He was not a traditional Catholic, but he was far more profoundly Catholic than I am, and more committed.

And Julien Green?

I saw him occasionally after the war, along with a whole group of writers. At that moment I had the strange impression that the mark of Cain had struck the French novelists of that generation: there was Mauriac with his cancer of the throat, his difficulty of speech; Malraux with his tics and those odd sneezes with which he punctuated his remarks; Daniel Rops half paralyzed; Gabriel Marcel, who could have been described as a dwarf. Post-War French literature appeared to me like a painting of Goya or Daumier.

Do you yourself regard faith as a disease or a blessing?

It would be a blessing if I were permanently conscious of it—which has never been the case. With age, though, doubt seems to gain the upper hand. It's my own fault. I've never been much of a religious person. There was a time, long ago, when I might have considered myself a practising Catholic. I still often go to Sunday mass, but I no longer feel at home, for reasons of my own—besides, the mass has changed considerably. It's no longer said in Latin; and all my education after my conversion was bound up with the mass in Latin. Even at Chungking in China I was able to attend a service I understood. Since the change to the vernacular, when I travel, I can't follow the Catholic services; they're in a different tongue each time. Nor do I care for the freedom given to priests to introduce endless prayers— for the astronauts or what have you—as they do at Antibes.

Do you go to Communion?

No, for I've broken the rules. They are rules I respect, so I haven't been to Communion now for nearly thirty years. The last time I went to Confession was at Phat Diem in Indo-China. I had been following the particularly murderous battles between the French paratroops and the Viet-Minh. The sight of so many corpses made me afraid. Fear drove me into the cathedral, around which the whole Catholic population was seeking refuge. The inhabitants had set up a whole lot of market stalls under the walls— they thought they'd be safer there.

So I went to find a Belgian priest I knew to hear my confession to the sound of gunfire (it was ten years since I had last confessed). He told me to say one Our Father and one Hail Mary. He also gave me one of the *Tintin* books to read as I had nothing else to hand.

What do you mean when you say you have 'broken the rules'?

(172)

In my private life, my situation is not regular. If I went to Communion, I would have to confess and make promises. I prefer to excommunicate myself. That's why I said, at a conference in Paris with Mauriac, that I could only speak in the name of the 'semi-lapsed', comparable in this respect with certain Communists who have reached the dangerous edge where faith wavers.

The priest in The Power and the Glory *also broke the rules, since he was father of a little girl, and he was a drunkard and fornicator, and yet . . .*

But he could always say mass. He was never stripped of that right.

While you, you are happy to torture yourself, are you not?

No, I became less depressive with age. I have, if you like, more doubts, but my faith has grown too. There's a difference between belief and faith. If I don't believe in X or Y, faith intervenes, telling me that I'm wrong not to believe. Faith is above belief. One can say that it's a gift of God, while belief is not. Belief is founded on reason. On the whole I keep my faith while enduring long periods of disbelief. At such moments I shrug my shoulders and tell myself I'm wrong—as though a brilliant mathematician had come and told me that my solution of an equation was wrong.   My faith remains in the background, but it remains.

So you are happy . . .

Not very. Who is?

Well then, at peace?

I'm just not bothered. I'll have it sorted out soon enough . . . or else I won't.

IX

'A Laugh in the Shadow of the Gallows'

'A laugh in the shadow of the gallows.' This was how a Swedish critic described Graham Greene when *Travels with my Aunt* came out. Laughter such as this cannot be delimited, it is a blend of so many contradictory elements. Humour is ever present in Graham Greene, prevailing over absurdity, holding death in check, affording an escape from the sorcery of success.

It is this laugh—sometimes impish, other times almost heroic—which is the genesis of the real Graham Greene, the one whose message is that it is not hope that quickens, but pain. This gives the pitiable Major Jones in *The Comedians* the strength to fight against the Tonton Macoutes knowing that he is going to be crushed. Maurice Castle, too, the double agent in *The Human Factor*, communicates an anguish which discredits accepted values: it reaffirms the painful mutual rejection of established societies and the individuals who lapse from them. And it is no doubt 'the shadow of the gallows' which gives to Graham Greene this insolent charisma of despair.

So the backcloth is not all that gay. Nonetheless, there is nobody who better enjoys a joke. Some years ago he came up with a quite straight-faced plan to found the Old Spies' Club, with subscriptions, pension fund, group photographs and so on. His youthful vitality also impelled him to set up another association, of people using France as a tax haven, in memory of Beau Brummel, who died at Caen in 1840. It was, he says, a fantastic farce, but the details were beginning to elude him. (The association folded up, he confesses, for lack of members.)

Childish pranks? No, important safety-valves, rather, as well as evidence of a facility for knowing how to profit from the playful aspects of life: no sooner does he find a Chu Chu on his path than he makes him a boon companion.

However, another character emerges from behind the jester, one who is bound to be considered less sympathetic by some, for he can be an irritant—this is the gad-fly. He reveals an obstinate anti-Americanism, to the point of seeming almost indulgent towards the Communists. There is a touch of provocation about some of his attitudes: this irresistible need to scandalize is familiar enough—it is a sort of quiet revenge.

The most disconcerting aspect of Graham Greene's laughter, however, resides in his attitude towards success. 'We simplify as we get older,' he writes in *The Quiet American*. Stylistically speaking he is of course right. But that seems to have little to do with his 'accidents of temperament'. After so many years of success, Graham Greene is still soliciting a sort of failure—without obtaining it. The superb creative detachment displayed by this man who is constantly cheating death, might it not be another way of laughing at posterity?

You are from every angle, including that of your private life (to which you so seldom allude), the opposite of a peaceful man. You have (or had) some very unorthodox tastes, which you present with a very British sense of litotes: the brothels of Havana under Batista left you as little dismayed as did certain other artificial heavens—and as did certain forms of dallying with death. Are you an 'old rascal'?

I expect I used to be. Today, I don't know .... It's true that I have a predilection for shady places. It enabled me, for instance, to understand Brighton and its seamy side. As a child, I was very fond of the place. When I went there to work on novels, I would read up all the news about the fights between rival gangs—for in those days knives and razor-blades were quickly drawn, particularly in the racing crowd.

One night, while I was planning to write *Brighton Rock*, I met one of the people from this set, a gangster from Wandsworth who had been slashed by his rivals, and in the small hours he took me off on his rounds. He even corrected my slang which he thought too austere and out-of-date. That was my only personal experience of the 'set'.

Would you agree that you like to find yourself in situations in which you can scoff at your enemies and defy the Establishment?

Yes, sometimes the need to do the opposite of what is expected of me is stronger than the threat of harm which may befall me if I go ahead.

In 1969 *The Sunday Telegraph* sent me to Paraguay. I took a boat at Buenos Aires to go up to Asuncion. Here at the British embassy, a message awaited me with a welcome from the President and a request that I contact Mr X from the Foreign Ministry; he would do his best to ensure that I enjoyed my stay and was enabled to visit the places I had in mind.

Shortly after my arrival, the pupils at a high school near my little hotel asked to meet me. I agreed in the conviction that I'd learn a good deal more about the country from them than I would from the Foreign Ministry 'guide'. They were accompanied by an interpreter, a horrible woman reminiscent of a Kapo from Belsen. There was no need for her presence, as I understood the questions and evidently the pupils understood my answers.

I spoke to them first about the encyclical on birth control *Humanae Vitae*, which the Pope had just addressed to Catholics (some of the pupils were sixteen-year-old girls). I advised them not to worry about the encyclical, for it would soon be forgotten. I tried to reassure them that it had little to do with Faith, and was not—as the Pope himself indicated—an infallible statement.

Then, as I knew that in spite of the absence of an official censorship the papers censored themselves, and that the slightest attack on the United States and the smallest allusion to Fidel Castro were forbidden, I asked the pupils if they'd be interested to hear a little about Fidel, whom I'd met two years previously in Havana. I spoke at some length about the Cuban leader.

After that my 'guide', who came every evening to my hotel for a drink with me, simply disappeared. He had promised me an aeroplane so that I could reach a place inaccessible by road, but I could no longer obtain the slightest official co-operation. Nobody recognized me any more; a wall had suddenly been raised between the Paraguayans and me. I was happy enough to leave the country with no worse difficulties than those.

Yesterday you told me that you played a small part in Truffaut's La Nuit Américaine. *That is so surprising in a person who has for years refused to show his face in public that I meant to ask you in what circumstances this happened.*

I didn't have to disguise myself. I was merely given an

umbrella which I had no use for as the scene was shot indoors. At any rate, no one knew who I was.

But surely you were recognized when the film came out?

The only person to recognize me was a woman-critic on *The New Yorker*. I should remark that my name wasn't listed among the credits. It gave me no little amusement because, as you say, it was not like me to do such a thing; but I could afford the odd touch of eccentricity. You see, I'd been a film critic, I'd co-produced a film with Mario Soldati, I'd written screenplays, but never had I been a film actor. I enjoyed completing my experience of the cinema.

Why do you refuse to appear on television?

Because I think it's not my business. I can think of too many writers who've become actors, even stars, on T.V. to the detriment of their work as writers. And yet, if one doesn't put oneself across on the screen, what's the point of appearing on it? So I'm unrepentant.

I have, though, once appeared secretly on television in a Hungarian documentary on Vietnam called 'A Letter to Graham Greene'; the camera more or less followed in the footsteps of *The Quiet American*.[1] Anyway, I appeared for a few moments to say a few words about my meeting with Ho Chi Minh, but on condition that they didn't sell the film to the West. They kept their promise. I made this gesture for a political reason as a protest against the Vietnam War. They showed the film on Vietnam's national day. I was quietly amused, imagining the faces at the American Embassy when they saw it.

---

[1] Graham Greene showed me, at Antibes, the hilarious dossier for *The Quiet American* as turned into a play by the Russians. He had attended one of the performances in Moscow in 1960 and had been offered this series of action-photos of the actors. The characters are cardboard cutouts, with fixed, stereotyped expressions. Graham Greene still laughs as he thumbs through the album.

You are a provocateur!

Little do you realize how I itch to give even freer rein to my instincts as troublemaker.

One day I did shamefully yield to temptation. Some Hamburg paper or other had asked me for an article on West Berlin. Before setting out[1] I decided that East Berlin would no doubt also deserve a little visit. But I didn't have a visa for East Berlin, and the Foreign Office had warned me that it would take me several months to obtain one, so I made an arrangement through a friend who was Rumanian ambassador in London: if I managed to be at Checkpoint Charlie, at the border between the British Zone of Berlin and East Germany, at a given date and time, a visa would be handed to me.

I had a pleasant trip in East Germany, partly thanks to a very agreeable guide, a Jewish bookseller who, paradoxically, had seen his family life destroyed because the wall had not been built soon enough. He'd married a woman who already had a son of fifteen or so. The boy habitually stole books from his step-father's library in order to exchange them in West Berlin against jeans and T-shirts. One day, when his entire edition of Shakespeare had vanished, my friend realized who was the culprit and threw such a fit of temper that his wife left him. 'So you see,' he said, 'if they'd built the wall a little faster, I wouldn't have lost my wife!'

It's these little paradoxes of life which amuse me, just as I was amused to climb onto the wall from the Eastern side and look at the Western camp through binoculars—as a rule one does the opposite.

In East Germany, during my brief stay of five days, an official gave me a list of CIA agents operating in West Berlin, with their addresses and telephone numbers. I

[1] In 1963.

(179)

publicized it by passing it to an English paper, just to make a little mischief again.

Are you not a dangerous man?

Oh, well, those agents—everyone knew about them already. I'd simply jumped at an opportunity to tease the CIA. This sort of prank does no harm to any individual.

And yet I imagine that you were a shy child.

I've always been shy. I still am. I suppose it shows because I try to conceal it. I put on an act for people I don't know. With women, I've usually needed to be shown the green light.

As a famous writer and dramatist who frequents the world of cinema, you would, one supposes, have been very much the centre of attention, much in demand. Have you ever been a playboy?

What kind of playboy? I've had a few adventures in my life, like everyone else. Each one has lasted quite a long time and I've stayed on excellent terms afterwards.

The End of the Affair *contains some very fine pages about 'human love, ordinary and corrupted'. Sexuality is omnipresent in your novels, but it often appears in disguise, devious, almost perverted—perverted by pity with Scobie, by success with Querry. In spite of certain passages in* The Comedians *the reader seldom comes upon scenes which are openly erotic. Is this due to your shyness, your modesty, or to a sort of puritanism?*

My novels written in the 'thirties—*Stamboul Train* for instance—were considered at the time slightly pornographic. They were not so to my mind. Since then, people's mentalities have evolved, and I don't think that anyone would ask me, as Maritain did, to cut this or that *risqué* scene.

The impression of glum or 'perverted' sensuality which

(180)

may perhaps lodge in your imagination derives, I think, from the way in which I presented it in *Brighton Rock*: the world is perceived there through the eyes of Pinkie, for whom the sexual act was a performance carried out on Saturday night in a sordid bedroom by parents who hadn't even taken the trouble, when he was very small, to put him to bed in another room (probably because they had no other room). This doesn't mean, of course, that I share Pinkie's viewpoint. After all, in *Travels with my Aunt*, love merges into Aunt Augusta's peals of laughter. Anyway, almost everything is sensuality; the way one holds a tea-cup is sometimes more revealing than the way one makes love.

'*We love even with our clothes, so that a sleeve can feel a sleeve*[1] ...'?

Yes. All the same pornography has no place in a serious book. As for my way of rendering sexuality, it has nothing to do with shyness. It's a purely technical problem. It's not the posture of people in bed which reveals their characters. You don't advance the story by giving details of their favourite positions. You merely attract the reader's attention towards very trivial points.

People who read Henry Miller, for example, expect to come upon this or that pornographic scene. It is not the characters that interest them but their own arousal. So they read on ever more quickly, hoping to come across the next pornographic passage. I think that Anthony Trollope evokes marvellously the passion and sensuality between Captain Burgo Fitzgerald and Lady Eustace[2] without having to write, 'I caressed her from breast to thigh'. Anyone can do that, and everyone knows how it's done.

[1] *The End of the Affair.*
[2] In *The Eustace Diamonds.*

That's why I have some reservations about porno-graphic literature.

'Pornographic' is perhaps too strong a word.

Not at all. It's the right word for Henry Miller. I've nothing against pornographic books as such, but don't let us call them literature.

For you, then, Henry Miller's novels are merely pornography?

I think that's their chief quality—in fact, their only good quality. Once he goes to work on philosophy or areas other than sex he tends to resemble a GI D. H. Lawrence.

In your last novel, Doctor Fischer of Geneva, *you obliquely and rather perversely revert to the game of Russian roulette : the narrator, who is seeking to die after the loss of his wife, accepts an invitation from the capricious millionaire, Doctor Fischer. At the end of the evening the guests move to a tub filled with presents—crackers all containing a huge cheque, all save one, into which the infernal Doctor Fischer says he has put a bomb. The guests take the risk—they are forewarned but greedy. The ending is bloody, even though in an access of cruelty you deprive your narrator of his own suicide.*

What is it that made you talk once again of this fascination of yours with 'the heart of darkness'?

It came naturally, with the narrative.

Like a nostalgia for the past?

No, but I doubt whether this story would have come to mind had Russian roulette not featured in my past. It's possible, as I was working on *Ways of Escape*, this collection of memories and *reportages*, that my memory helped me with the plot of *Doctor Fischer*.

One way for you to be finally rid of that past . . .

I don't think I can ever be rid of it. I don't particularly want to be rid of the past—at least not of that one.

Not even of the terrible Russian roulette episode?

(182)

No: I find it interesting, not terrible. And curious that, at the time, even Russian roulette finally bored me.

You do not feel any retrospective fear?

No. I've told you that I couldn't start again today. Besides, I'm not afraid any more—that's the real bore.

Perhaps your fear has become less personal, less egocentric. I was wondering whether your constant alertness to what is going on around you has finally left you free to look at yourself with greater serenity.

I still hate looking myself in the face. I've succeeded in proving to myself that I've become a reasonably good writer. That's enough for me.

But what is happening in the world at present impairs any serenity I may have acquired. I believe—without being totally convinced—that we're heading for a Third World War; that at all events we're going through a very dangerous time.

I dreamt last night that a huge aircraft landed, carrying German troops. Then a very polite officer interrogated me. One felt already in occupied territory. Of course in reality one would expect to see Russian not German soldiers landing—but this dream certainly indicates the threat we feel under at present.

Do you still cherish such values as patriotism?

Yes. I think one great danger comes from treachery, the defection of secret service agents. The 'turning' of a KGB man, for instance, would never surprise me, because the profession can become a sort of game as abstract as chess: the spy takes more interest in the mechanics of his calling than in its ultimate goal—the defence of his country. The 'game' (a serious game) achieves such a degree of sophistication that the player loses sight of his moral values.

I can understand a man's temptation to turn double

agent, for the game becomes more interesting. Perhaps my childhood experience of divided loyalties has helped me to sympathize with people like Kim Philby, who have gone to the limit with their divided loyalties. I myself would not be capable of such courage, of such a force of conviction.

So you do not think, as Andrew Boyle implies in his book where he speaks precisely of the Cambridge spies—Philby, Burgess, Mclean and others—that espionage is one of the less honourable professions?

If a person risks his life fighting for a cause, I don't see how one can make such an idiotic judgement. In time of war, espionage is an essential weapon. Not far from me in the South of France lived one of the double agents who served our cause to great effect during the war. His name was Popov. He was a Jugoslav. He was sent to England by the German secret service, but he was already working for us. From time to time he returned to Lisbon to report to his chiefs. It was thanks to him that we had sight of a questionnaire furnished by the Japanese to the Germans, which indicated that they were preparing the attack on Pearl Harbor. He passed these documents to Hoover who, unfortunately, left them in a drawer.

In peacetime I don't see why espionage should be any more disreputable than in war. Spies (other than those in books) earn very little. They generally risk their necks out of idealism, and quite clear-sightedly.

How did you react to the invasion of Afghanistan?

It's odd, but it didn't shock me as much as the invasion of Czechoslovakia or Hungary, for the Communist regime in office was a dreadful one. Amin was a bloodthirsty Stalinist. The Vietnamese invasion of Cambodia didn't shock me either. Pol Pot and Amin were monsters who did nothing but bring discredit on Communism. But don't go thinking that I'm in favour of the invasion of Afghanistan. I merely say that it doesn't shock me. One way or another something must serve as a warning to the USSR not to go too far: I do think we're risking a nuclear conflict.

On which side would you be?

One would have no time to choose. On the other hand I believe that West Germany can easily become a battle-ground in which conventional weapons would be used.

And in that case, where would you stand?

In the Western camp. Not if we invaded the USSR, only if the USSR invaded the German Federal Republic.

Do you regard yourself as a pessimist or an optimist?

I don't know. My English critics find my vision of the world very pessimistic. The French, on the other hand, find a good deal of optimism in my books. In everyday life I'm inclined to be ready when trouble comes (as Housman wrote). That's my temperament.

In the 'Personal Postscript' to your Collected Essays you say, 'For a writer as much as for a priest there is no such thing as success.' What do you mean?

Well, there *is* no such thing as success. The priest can't hope to become a saint—or else it's an illusory dream which vanishes with time; the writer can't hope to write a book to equal those of Tolstoy, Dickens or Balzac. He might have dared to believe in the possibility at the outset, but his books always carry a flaw somewhere.

Then what is it that we call 'success'?

That's very simple: for me, 'success' would mean writing a very good book.

Do you not believe that you have already achieved this, even unwittingly?

I have not succeeded in writing the book I want to write.

Is this what keeps you going?

Well ... maybe.

Are you dissatisfied with yourself?

Not with myself, with my talent.

Which explains your periodic moods of despair.

Yes. My desk is littered with unfinished books—still-born books. Failures.

You might consider them, rather, as the fruit of an enormous creativity.

By no means. Compared with the giants my creativity is pitiful.

Is not your sin quite simply one of pride?

Why? Because I've failed? Is it pride, to fail?

I may be mistaken, but you resemble Scobie a little: you ask too much of yourself.

If the writer's occupation merely represented a means of earning a living, one would write nothing. Without the ambition to be a good writer, one wouldn't go on. Where, then, is the pride? A painter always expects to surpass himself, to accomplish his masterpiece.

But you are famous. Everyone reads your books. Looked at this way, you really have 'failed at failure'!

There was a time in France when everybody read Charles Morgan. I'm a good enough writer. Better than many. I'm not proud but realistic. I'm not modest, either. But I can't place myself among the giants. Anyway, it's too late ... I'm at least a hundred and ten years old!

Why a hundred and ten?

I've taken this figure at random, but it seems to me impossible to have lived through all I have in seventy-six years. And yet ...

A writer's old age can be very strange. Sometimes it's like his books: Evelyn Waugh, who had made such fun of Apthorpe's 'thunder-box', died in the w.c. Zola, like the miners in *Germinal*, was suffocated by charcoal fumes, and now, at the age of seventy-six, I find myself at grips with the criminal '*milieu*' of Nice—but I hope that I, at any rate, shall get the better of Pinkie.